Glasgow's
BLYTHSWOOD

GRAEME SMITH

Glasgow's New Town of Blythswood

Two wise owls keeping watch on St Vincent Street, successors to the partridges and hares on Blythswood Hill.

CHARING CROSS

ELMBANK STREET

HOLLAND STREET

PITT STREET

M8 MOTORWAY
RAMPS

A R G Y L E

R I V E R

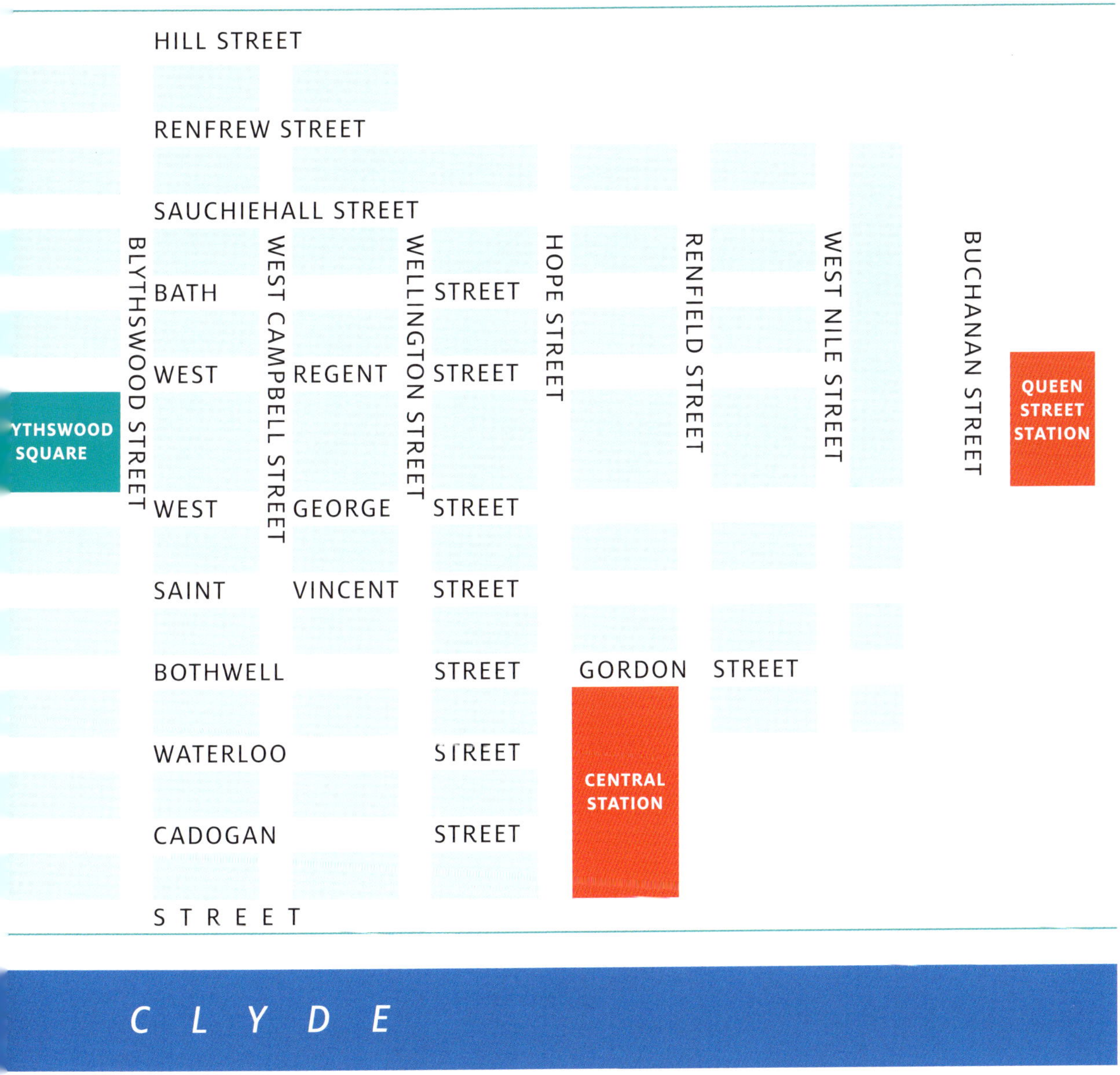

HILL STREET

RENFREW STREET

SAUCHIEHALL STREET

BLYTHSWOOD STREET

WEST CAMPBELL STREET

WELLINGTON STREET

HOPE STREET

RENFIELD STREET

WEST NILE STREET

BUCHANAN STREET

BATH STREET

WEST REGENT STREET

QUEEN STREET STATION

YTHSWOOD SQUARE

WEST GEORGE STREET

SAINT VINCENT STREET

BOTHWELL STREET

GORDON STREET

WATERLOO STREET

CENTRAL STATION

CADOGAN STREET

STREET

CLYDE

A Personal Note

As a schoolboy I had a Saturday job and holiday job with Marks & Spencer's in Sauchiehall Street, with Garnethill behind it. As warehouse boys we replenished the fruit counters by loading up huge trolleys with all sorts of fruit from the upper warehouse. Much sampling of fruit took place as we took the heavy trolleys down in the slow lift to the ground floor. Marks' staff canteen was superb with a three course lunch for sixpence. At closing time on Saturday some fruit walked out the door, which my girlfriend Jean (future wife) and I enjoyed as we went off to various venues.

The peaches were delicious!

I got to know Blythswood Hill in the 1960s when I served my apprenticeship at 200 St Vincent Street with the firm of Reid & Mair, chartered accountants. On Friday evenings once the lecture classes ended at the CA Institute at 218-220 St Vincent Street hundreds of apprentices (men mainly) scaled out – some meeting girlfriends at the door – and went off to hostelries towards West Nile Street. For Jean and I, Danny Brown's at 79 St Vincent Street was a good end to the working week and a good start for the weekend.

I must add that this Smith family is not related to the Smiths of Blythswood Square, nor to Madeleine.

[signature]

By the Same Author
The Theatre Royal: Entertaining a Nation
Alhambra Glasgow

Co-author
Newton Mearns Through Time

Contributor and Co-editor
The University of Glasgow Library – Friendly Shelves

Contributor
Ships for a Nation – John Brown's of Clydebank
Arthur Lloyd compendium of Theatres and Music Halls in Britain and Ireland

Glasgow's

BLYTHSWOOD

Graeme Smith

www.blythswoodsmith.co.uk

Hallway of one of the townhouses which comprise the Royal College of Physicians and Surgeons of Glasgow, St Vincent Street.

Contents

Glasgow's Blythswood – an Introduction 8

The New Town in the city 14

William Harley

1 William Harley and Jane Laird –
   Family Time 18
2 Cotton Business 26
3 Schools for All 32
4 Blythswood Pleasure Gardens 38
5 Promoting the Observatory 48
6 Harley's Water 54
7 Harley's Baths in Bath Street 58
8 Harley's Byres and Willowbank Dairy 64
9 Harley's Willowbank Baking Company 72
10 The Campbells and Douglases
   of Blythswood 76

Blythswood and Garnethill

11 Planning it out 82
12 First New Houses 86
13 The Blair Family and
   242 St Vincent Street 94
14 Money Matters and the
   Smith Family 102
15 Blythswood Square 106
16 The Royal Scottish Automobile Club 116

Blythswood Holm

17 James Scott and Jane Galbraith 124
18 Bothwell Street 130
19 West to St Vincent Crescent 144
20 Elmbank Crescent and Its Cousins 152

An A to Z of Streets 164
   Bath Street 166
   Blythswood Square 174
   Blythswood Street 180
   Bothwell Street 182
   Douglas Street 190
   Elmbank Street 192
   Gordon Street 194
   Hill Street 198
   Holland Street 200
   Hope Street 202
   Pitt Street 206
   Renfield Street 208
   Renfrew Street 212
   St Vincent Street 214
   Sauchiehall Street 226
   Waterloo Street 232
   Wellington Street 236
   West Campbell Street 238
   West George Street 240
   West Nile Street 248
   West Regent Street 252

Acknowledgements 258
   Selected Reading 260

Cover Illustrations
St Vincent Street skyline/Salon de Luxe, Willow Tearooms, Sauchiehall Street/Blythswood Square gardens/West George Street viewing up Blythswood Hill. (Front inside) Waterloo Street /(Rear inside) Sauchiehall Street.

Glasgow's Blythswood – an Introduction

West George Street on Blythswood Hill, viewing up to Blythswood Square.

In style and confidence Glasgow streaked ahead. *Blythswood* is well named – meaning bright and pleasing – and vistas everywhere. In the 1790s, west of the new houses in Buchanan Street lay countryside – open fields and a few hedge rows, some market gardens and cabbage patches, hares and partridges. Soon the grid-iron street pattern pioneered around George Square would expand west across Blythswood Hill, Garnet Hill and Woodside Hill complemented by crescents and gardens. Likewise, south of the river Clyde the same pattern forming Tradeston, Laurieston and Hutchesontown. By the 1820s Glasgow was the largest city in Scotland and very soon would become the largest in Europe after London, Paris, Berlin, Vienna and St. Petersburg.

The magnificent New Town of Blythswood

From Sauchiehall Street to Bothwell Street, and below, and west from Buchanan Street up Blythswood Hill and its slope down to Elm Bank, emerged 'The magnificent New Town of Blythswood' crowned by the elegance of Blythswood Square. From 1800 onwards residential terraces of Georgian townhouses and Victorian palazzos lined the slopes. Leisure gardens and squares formed beyond the town's

Fashions for June, The Looking Glass, 1825.

then boundary, Enoch Burn. Also named as the Glasgow Burn, it tumbled south past the newly built St Enoch's Square into the Clyde. By far, Blythswood became the wealthiest and healthiest part of the expanding city. The oldest surviving villa is of 1819 in St Vincent Street and continues as the central part of the Royal College of Physicians and Surgeons of Glasgow, founded by Maister Peter Lowe in 1599.

The spacious townhouses of two or three storeys, and sporadic villas, all had basement rooms sometimes used as offices for the occupant's business. The wide streets were laid with granite stones and setts, with broad Caithness flagstone pavements. Roofing slates from North Wales were shipped in from Liverpool and very soon from the slate quarries near Oban.

Blythswood New Town was largely completed by the 1850s. Later decades saw townhouse extensions and conversions. Prosperity brought exquisite Victorian palaces of commerce growing skyward, joined today by modern cousins. Churches, schools, clubs, hotels and artists' studios joined the community, with around its edges some theatres and tenements.

Its buildings are chiefly of white sandstone, followed by red sandstone, with some marble and granite. Over time the streets of Blythswood have become a distinguished part of the commercial life of Glasgow, while most recently residential use is returning.

To ensure desirable residences with fresh air and panoramic views the new Blythswood development banned industry, although one proposal in 1829 to build a railway from

Sunshine in Blythswood Square, a panorama of the terrace on the east-side.

West George Street with a little night rain.

St Rollox (Springburn), including tunnelling under Blythswood Square, down to the Broomielaw to export Lanarkshire coal came close to being built. Some land bought on Blythswood Holm by the railway companies later found use in and around the new Central Station.

The Lands of Blythswood

After the Reformation, the common-grazing Lands of Blythswood and, on the south side of the Clyde, the Lands of Gorbals were purchased by the Elphinstone family, one of the earliest merchant families of Glasgow. From the 1420s they exported cured salmon and herrings to France and the Baltic and imported brandy, wines and salt; and iron and timber from the Baltic. One of them, Provost Sir George Elphinstone, became the member for Glasgow in the Scots Parliament, later becoming the Lord Justice Clerk. On his passing in 1634 the impecunious knight's lands were bought by Robert Douglas of Mains, who had married George's daughter and heiress. When

A merchant house and offices in West George Street, classical and confident.

he in turn was bankrupted the vast lands on both sides of the Clyde were bought in 1640 by the Town Council, Trades House and Hutchesons' Hospital to be held for the public good. Property and politics, however, intertwined as did the Douglas and Campbell families. A Douglas family member, Colin Campbell, of Argyll stock, became Provost of the city as did his son who purchased the Lands of Blythswood, which extended to the River Kelvin, from the Town Council for a mere fraction, a wanworth, of their real value.

In 1792 the Campbells obtained an Act of Parliament changing the conditions of ownership to let them sell land adjacent to the city for development: in the words of the preamble 'to the great beauty and advantage of the town and the benefit of John Campbell and other heirs'. The Douglas-Campbells of Blythswood and not the Common Good represented by the Town Council – became immensely wealthy when they started to sell portions to developers and amass the annual feu-duty rentals. In Scotland they reached the eminence, if not the total wealth, of the Grosvenor family of London.

William Harley and his successors

The first major developer was the textile manufacturer and public-spirited pioneer William Harley who opened up Bath Street, St Vincent

Street, West Nile Street, West George Street, West Regent Street, Blythswood Square and the edges of Garnet Hill along Renfrew Street. The Sauchie Haugh road, once a country lane leading to Partick, would emerge as Sauchiehall Street.

He also laid out pleasure grounds and a viewing tower at the top of Blythswood Hill, equally known then as Harley's Hill, and created the city's first piped water supply, together with the first public indoor swimming baths in Scotland, complete with its own coffee house. He built the largest and first hygienic dairy, and provided milk deliveries to each district. A bakery was added with its goods for sale in the city and other towns along the Clyde and in Belfast. By way of international recognition he was invited by the Tsar of Russia to organise the Imperial Dairy of the new summer palaces near St Petersburg.

The second major developer was calico-printer James Scott – who was also aware of his civic duty towards forming new parks – most notably Kelvingrove – promoting new railways and docks and bringing fresh water from Loch Katrine. He started the construction of Bothwell Street, built a viaduct at Bothwell Circus, and created, further west, St Vincent Crescent – one of the first crescents in the city – Corunna Street and Minerva Street next to the first site of the Royal Botanic Gardens at Sandyford Toll. He went on to be an oil merchant and colleague of Dr James 'Paraffin' Young who started the oil industry.

Enjoy this panorama of people and places, the story of its streets and buildings, its tapestry of architecture, and the colour and essence of two centuries of being 'the New Town of Blythswood'.

A Guide

Blythswood presently comprises the finest domestic accommodation in Glasgow: commodious houses owned for the most part by the Glasgow Nabobs. Except for the steeper slopes, the basic ingredient is a short terrace three storeys high, often with a centrepiece and end pavilions. Pilasters are frequently to be seen, and some porches. The cornices tend to be emphatic, and the stone is ashlar.

Servants are required for the running of such houses. There is a ready supply of girls from the Highlands to meet the demand. At the current rates, wages, including live-in lodging and food are: for a cook, £16 per annum; for a tablemaid, housemaid or laundrymaid, £12 per annum; and for a gardener, 15 shillings per week.

From 'An Illustrated Guide to Glasgow 1837'

Bothwell Street from Blythswood Street.

The ceremonial hall of the Royal College of Physicians and Surgeons of Glasgow, St Vincent Street.

Blythswood Square gardens, the idea of William Harley.

The New Town in the City

Top: Glasgow's Broomielaw and shipping on the Clyde, gateway to the world, painting by Robert Salmon, 1832.
Bottom: *Awfu weather*, The Looking Glass, 1825.

International trade and new investments

Scotland's dominance in Atlantic trades and significance in the East India Company now extended to China and Australia. As an early English writer noted: 'We are not surprised to find a host of Scotchmen on whatever shore we may step, where money is to be made. Neither the snows of Canada nor the heats of India present any obstacles to them'. This was the background to the huge expansion of Glasgow. Throughout the eighteenth century Glasgow was the fastest growing town in Scotland, even before the start of the Industrial Revolution. Through industry, art and science it became the largest city in Scotland and very soon would be the Second City of Empire.

From its early days, over 1500 years ago, and becoming a burgh in 1175 and royal burgh in 1611 – when it was also granted 'freedom of the river from Broomilaw to the Cloch' three miles downstream from Greenock – the historic centre stretched north from the shallow crossing over the Clyde. From Glasgow Cross and Glasgow Green the centre rose past the University in the High Street to the Cathedral. Its first planned New Town, creating George Square and its grid of streets, was in progress by the 1780s. By 1800, the west side of Buchanan Street was gradually being built on.

The choice of wide streets all at right angles to each other was confirmed after the council, through Provost Campbell of Blythswood, met in 1792 with architect John Craig, winner of the competition for the first layout style of Edinburgh's New Town.

The area of Blythswood would be Glasgow's second New Town. Glasgow's grid-iron system was adopted in New York in 1811, and later in Chicago.

Politics and parliament

Colin Campbell of Blythswood became Provost and his brother and successor Archibald Campbell was the Member of Parliament for Glasgow and adjacent burghs for a number of years. Always a powerful conservative in politics, he did not support the Reform movement and did not vote in favour of the abolition of slavery. However in 1838 an obituarist commented on 'the hilarity which beamed from his bland countenance'. His rival in politics was the radical and energetic Kirkman Finlay, a later Provost and President of the Glasgow Chamber of Commerce founded in 1783. He defeated Campbell to become Glasgow MP for a period from 1812. Head of the house of James Finlay & Co, famed for their cottons, woollens, and later its tea growing, he was the leading merchant in Britain who brought to an end the monopoly held by the Honourable East India Company which was preventing others from trading with India and China. And earlier than that he broke Napoleon's continental blockade of trade from Britain by helping to capture the isles of Heligoland and trading from there, and from Gibraltar and Malta, to the countries beyond.

The planning and building of Blythswood started in earnest in 1800. All of its vast lands lay outside the town's royal-burgh boundaries. In 1830 the council moved its boundaries west to the river Kelvin, even though Campbell had petitioned Parliament in 1818 to make

Kirkman Finlay, leading international merchant and statesman, engraving of a painting by John Graham Gilbert.

View of Glasgow Green and a Passing Storm, painting by John Knox about 1818, with Nelson's Monument in the foreground, erected in 1806.

Blythswood a burgh in its own right but met opposition from its new residents. Perhaps to assuage the public, Colin Campbell and Henry Monteith obtained a royal charter in 1825 to erect a theatre in Blythswood, but it was not built. Landlords and property developers around Glasgow Cross campaigned against any westerly expansion. Instead, they demanded new public buildings to be built in the centre of the city and on its east-side. They were rewarded with the new Town Hall and the High Court being built facing Glasgow Green.

It made civic sense for the Blythswood residents to be within the enlarged burgh including now the benefit of the Glasgow police force created in 1800, the first public police force in Britain. Before then the residents, including William Harley himself, took turns to support the night watchmen employed, and to keep them awake!

Houses and shops

In the tradition of Robert Adam some mason/ architects also designed furniture, such as Alexander 'Greek' Thomson, to be followed by Charles Rennie Mackintosh. A publisher in 1812 writes: 'Woodwork is extensively done in all its branches within the city, particularly that of cabinet making which is in general executed in a style of exquisite elegance and taste'.

In the first fifty years of the nineteenth century the finest furniture firms included Cleland, Jack, Paterson & Co. in Trongate. A son James Cleland and business partner William Jack were also builders and property developers on Blythswood Hill on steadings bought from William Harley. James Cleland became the city's esteemed Superintendent of Public Works. Another such firm was John Reid & Co. of Buchanan Street whose son and business partner Robert Reid assumed the nom-de-plume of Senex for his highly readable books on the growth of Glasgow in his lifetime. John Reid & Co. were the largest importers and wholesalers of mahogany in Scotland, and sold across Britain. Archibald Gardner & Son of Jamaica Street gained renown for their mahogany with quality inlays. And Robert Wylie and William Lochhead became the largest firm of all, with their galleried warehouse showrooms in Buchanan Street. Wylie & Lochhead much later became a central part of the nationwide House of Fraser headquartered in the city. Among numerous carpet weavers, James Templeton & Co., next to Glasgow Green, started business and soon became Britain's largest firm of carpet manufacturers.

Drapery, household goods and decoration were supplied from many warehouses. Scotch, Brussels [velvet] and Turkish carpets, rugs and other floorcoverings were available. Paper hangings and paint in a range of colours were in good supply. For the very wealthy, the hand-painted paper hangings from China were the desired items for some main rooms. These were available, along with oriental silks, following the return of sea captains of the Hon. East India Company who brought them back from the Orient as part of their cargo share of trading.

As new houses were built and families moved ever westward so too did shops, all known then as warehouses. The distance became too great from the markets clustered near the Cross such as the meal market, cheese market and fish market and 'the beef, mutton and vegetable markets in King Street are comparatively deserted' by the

Inside the furniture warehouse of Cleland, Jack, Paterson & Co. in the Trongate, 1812.

1830s. Retail food shops opened in the streets leading to Jamaica Street, and the markets would soon become wholesalers.

Room heating and cooking on kitchen ranges were fuelled by the plentiful supply of coal from numerous mines in and close to the city. Hardware, china and cutlery came from arcades and warehouses. Initially lighting was by oil and penny candles. Gas street lighting was introduced gradually from the 1820s and electricity for use in public buildings from the 1890s.

In the 1820s Dorothy Wordsworth upon sailing into Glasgow by steamer records:

Landed at Glasgow in the twilight – great bustle in the harbour – puffing of steamboats – masts of ships all along the shore. Taverns, houses and shops are all fronting the water – lamp-lighting was begun: and before I reached the Trongate, twilight was gone, and the shops shining in full splendour. Streets were very busy – not with carriages, but people – posting away, like Londoners, as if they had more business than time.

Chapter 1

William Harley and Jane Laird – Family Time

Greenock and the Clyde, viewing upriver to Port Glasgow and Dumbarton, towards Glasgow, painting by Robert Salmon, 1816.

William Harley, engraving by Robert Scott from a portrait in the 1820s, possibly by George Watson.

William Harley, born in 1767 in Glendevon to tenant farmer James Harley and his wife Helena Blyd, daughter of a neighbouring farmer, was orphaned at a young age and was brought up by his grandmother.

He served his apprenticeship as a thread draw-boy and weaver in the fine-linen satinette works of his mother's brother in nearby Kinross. He then joined the same uncle's brown-linen works in Perth where he learned the skills of buying and selling.

By the 1770s Glasgow was Britain's centre for manufacturing linen, nature's strongest fibre. In 1783 Glasgow founded its Chamber of Commerce, the first major chamber in Britain, promoting its international commerce and quality of goods. New technologies in spinning, weaving, bleaching, dyeing and printing were applied in the 1780s onwards to the more lucrative and comfortable cotton wool. Soon there were 134 cotton mills in Scotland, mostly in and around Glasgow. Cotton was King. In 1789 William Harley headed off to Glasgow and would become one of its many millionaires.

Family network

In 1801 the jovial William married **Jane Laird** daughter of a Greenock merchant John Laird who headed John Laird & Sons rope and sailcloth manufacturers. Their ropeworks were on an extensive scale and they had their own quay which later made way for the town's Albert Harbour and Prince's Pier. The family home was Glebe House next to the ropeworks. Jane's grandfather John, a shipbroker and flax importer, had developed the firm and become Provost of Greenock. He was a friend of the evangelist John Wesley. In 1794 when invasion by France was a real threat Jane's father placed his vast sail loft at the disposal of the military for use as a hospital.

Her brother Alexander Laird was a passenger on the first voyage of Henry Bell's famous *PS Comet* in 1812 on the Clyde, the first sailing of a seagoing steamship in Europe. He would soon start the first steam shipping lines from Greenock and Glasgow, the Laird Lines – linking the Clyde, Ireland and Liverpool where their

The emblem of Glasgow Chamber of Commerce is the flying stork (carrying flax) representing Oriental good fortune and longevity.

Glendevon, near Kinross.

Greenock, about 1800, showing Fort Jervis with Lairds' Ropeworks and Quay behind. Glebe House is on the left.

Henry Bell's *PS Comet* on the Clyde, 1812.

MV Royal Scotsman of the later Burns & Laird fleet in the 1960s.

brother William now stayed. The shipping company later became Burns & Laird. William had been sent by their father to open a base on the Mersey to increase their business in rope and canvas. But once there the Lairds expanded into ironworks, shipbuilding and engine-building creating John Laird & Company in Birkenhead facing over to Liverpool. In the twentieth century the company became Cammell Laird. One of Jane's nephews McGregor Laird became the first secretary of the Cunard Line and a founder of the Elder Dempster Line with its pioneering trade with West Africa.

Their family of four sons and six daughters, all having Laird as their middle name, were taught by tutors and governesses at their home, Willowbank – just north-west of today's Blythswood Square – and when older were sent to a Moravian School in Germany. Mrs Harley died in 1818, when her husband was in the midst of his financial troubles over the development of Blythswood.

Civic life and the Tsar

William Harley became a member of the court of directors of the new Royal Infirmary built in 1794 close to the Cathedral. He was a founder of the Glasgow Astronomical Sciences Society. Back on *terra firma*, Harley was also a member of the (Royal) Highland Society of Scotland. He was active in church matters, including the new Tabernacle on the west side of Jamaica Street where the Volunteers used to drill their horses. He also promoted schooling for children. In the poorest areas fewer than 6% attended any type of school. Harley assisted Sabbath schools and opened two new schools.

North-west corner of Blythswood Square beyond which was Willow Bank, residence of the Harleys.

In the decades when many churches in Scotland and England rested on their oars, and were subject to overview by a Government alarmed by the cry for parliamentary democracy, he joined the Haldane brothers of Airthrey near Stirling, and others, in one of their annual summer missions to country areas to renew congregational life. Over two months in 1800, starting by mail-coach from the Tontine to Port Glasgow, they travelled to the towns and villages of the Firth of Clyde and Kintyre. Their preaching and evangelical work attracted large attendances including many who felt marginalised, including Gaelic speakers. In a few places their evangelist zeal was looked down on by the minister of the established church and in Inveraray near the end of the summer tour the Sheriff threatened to imprison them unless they took the oath of allegiance. Government was anxious about dissent and invasion threats from republican France. The pioneering Haldanes helped create numerous congregational churches, seminars and Sabbath-evening schools throughout Britain and Ireland.

The Royal Infirmary, Glasgow, original building of 1794.

In his later years in the 1820s William Harley lived for the most part in Dunoon, as an unpaid evangelist, and ensuring the town's night soil was collected each day and turned into manure at his farm nearby. He completed his book on agricultural improvement and modern dairies – *The Harleian Dairy System* – published in 1829, which sold across Britain and Ireland into the 1850s. He published a prospectus in London announcing his plan to open a baking establishment there, similar to his Glasgow one. The last entry for William Harley in the Glasgow

Tsar Nicholas I of Russia, portrait by Franz Krüger.

Directory of 1828 reads – 'Letters to be left at John Laird & Co, 79 Miller Street.'

It was when his youngest son, Henry, was completing his education in London that an invitation came from Tsar Nicholas I, an engineer by profession, inviting William Harley to travel to Russia. The Tsar had decided to appoint him to superintend and improve the new Imperial Dairy being built in St Petersburg close to the new Summer Palaces. It is thought that the Tsar commissioned Harley's portrait in advance of the journey. Sadly, when starting his travel, Harley collapsed and died in London in May 1830, aged 63.

Sons, daughters and Switzerland

Of their family, James became general manager of the Willow Bank Baking Company before settling in Liverpool; John and William went to New Brunswick, Canada where William became a customs officer; and young Henry Laird Harley became a 1st Engineer in the Hon. East India Company's navy, which in the Orient was equal to the Royal Navy. His ship was the first iron warship in the world (and opium carrier) *Nemesis*, appropriately built by his cousin John at Lairds of Birkenhead. It was one of a number being built by them for the Secret Committee of the East India Company, and was commanded by Captain

The warship *Nemesis* in action in the China Seas at Canton River.

(later Admiral) William Hutcheon Hall who had studied steam engines in Glasgow. The Chinese described her as 'the devil ship' and placed a bounty of 50,000 dollars on her capture or purchase. In an early encounter in the wars with China in the 1840s his ship was surrounded by a fleet of forty Chinese war-junks attempting to capture it but *Nemesis* emerged victorious.

The three eldest daughters Janet, Helen and Mary, started a subscription academy in Falkirk and later one in Alloa. After their father's death they removed to Glasgow. They took over an academy in Newton Place and moved it to No 1 Claremont Terrace where for many years the Misses Harley conducted and expanded their institution for young ladies. Under its full name of the West of Scotland Institution for the Board and Education of Young Ladies it attracted pupils from around Scotland. Sometimes referred to as Claremont Terrace Academy it also enrolled weekly boarders, later starting a primary class for boys up to age eight. Engaging about seventeen teachers, in addition to governesses, it taught English, History, Geography, Scripture, Modern Languages (French, German and Italian), Mathematics, Needlework, Drawing, Deportment and Music – one of the music teachers, Julius Seligmann, was a founder of the Scottish National Orchestra. The dancing teacher was a former ballet master at Covent Garden, Charles D'Albert. Fees were 22 guineas a season, and down to 6 guineas for the younger entrants. Fees for full boarders were around 45 guineas, and their laundress 5 guineas.

No 1 Claremont Terrace housed the Misses Harley's School for Young Ladies.

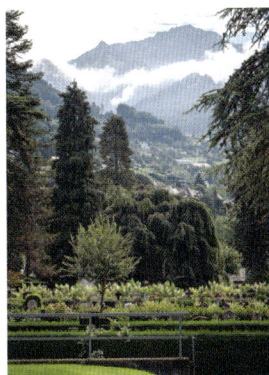

Montreux with the Alps above and Clarens Cemetery in the foreground.
Overleaf: Greenock and the Clyde viewing upriver to Port Glasgow and Dumbarton, towards Glasgow, painting by Robert Salmon, 1816.

In the summer months each year the sisters travelled with some of their pupils to a house in Montreux on the shores of Lake Geneva. On retiring, they settled in Switzerland, where they held a weekly Bible Reading in their home in Montreux and ministered to the poor and the sick. They successfully petitioned the Free Church of Scotland and a Free Church seated for 200, and complete with a house and library, opened in Montreux from 1867 onwards attracting congregations made up of some twelve nationalities. Of the children of Jane and William Harley the last daughter Elizabeth Laird Harley passed on in Switzerland in 1906.

Chapter 2

Cotton Business

Portrait of a Young Lady, complete with shawl, painting by E.F.Leybold, 1824.

Harley was a 'wee cork', a master weaver or tradesman who expanded business starting as an agent or go-between by contracting work out. He would ensure that yarn was supplied, the pattern specified and the finished material collected. The wee corks were very active in Glasgow and in Paisley.

In Glasgow two of the most prominent started as hand loom weavers – David Dale who established powered cotton spinning mills around the west of Scotland including his pioneering village of New Lanark (which is now a UNESCO World Heritage centre) and James Monteith, the son of a market gardener in Anderston, who with his sons introduced fine muslin and the most advanced power-loom weaving factories. Another master weaver was Charles Tennant, the radical reformer, who settled in Glasgow and discovered how to make bleach for textiles on an industrial scale. He established his chemical works in St Rollox, just beyond Sighthill, which became the largest chemical works in the world.

David Dale, painting by Hugh William Williams.

Fine muslin and gingham became Glasgow specialities dominating Britain's trade in these sectors. In Paisley, of its wee corks some changed through the nineteenth century from making

New Lanark in 1818, painting by its resident art teacher John Winning.

Anderston viewed from the Clyde, with Anderston Brewery centre left and Henry Houldsworth's Cotton Work on the right. Drawing by James Hopkirk, 1820s.

Display of textiles, 1914, made by D & J Anderson Ltd, Atlantic Mills, Bridgeton.

George Square, with St Vincent Street stretching up Blythswood Hill, engraving by Joseph Swan, 1829.

fancy fabrics and shawls to become cotton thread manufacturers, with the Clark and Coats families becoming the largest manufacturers of sewing thread in the world.

'Hotch-potch huxter, Laird o'Willowbank'

Harley's manufacturing business and warehouse was in the customary trades of shirtings, sheetings, towellings, damasks, shawls and dress goods, notably in the weaving and embellishment of muslin, gingham, and possibly silk. Glasgow was famous at home and abroad for producing these lightweight materials for women's and children's dresses, gingham being introduced here first and usually in blue and white colours with the new turkey red adding to the choice. Harley sold widely at home and abroad. George Sands, one of the weaver poets of the city, writes of him as 'The hotch-potch huxter, Laird o'Willowbank.'

Very likely, Harley's hand loom weavers were in Anderston or Cowcaddens or else in the town's largest weaving districts Calton and Bridgeton, either working at home or in loom sheds and small factories of up to six looms. The purr and click of weaving shuttles could be heard from morning till dusk. Weavers' houses were usually of two storeys, the family living upstairs and the loom-shop downstairs. Gingham and muslin weavers were in the majority. Carpet weavers were the highest paid. Thousands of needlewomen were employed in the Glasgow area to meet the needs of so many businesses and households.

To ensure his right to trade and promote his business William Harley became a member of the Merchants House which then was in the Briggait near Stockwell Street.

In the 1790s he joined forces with manufacturer Ninian McGilp, trading as Harley & McGilp from their warehouse near George Square until 1806 when McGilp set up on his own in Montrose Street – and in the 1820s buying a house in the new Renfield Street – before retiring to Rhu. Harley continued as William

Hand loom weaver, drawing by James Hopkirk, 1820s.

Harley & Company from 1806 to 1816 in a new warehouse in South Frederick Street.

No person better known

With his novel ventures on Blythswood Hill and his establishment there supplying piped water, baths, milk and dairy produce, bread and baking Harley was a popular man.

The writer Robert Reid, better known as 'Senex', describes him well:

> No person that walked the streets of Glasgow was better known. He was always dressed the same – a blue coat with gilt buttons, drab breeches and leggings, a voluminous white neckcloth in which his chin was sunk (the fashion of the French in '93), and a broad-rimmed hat, completed his outward man. Not a bad resemblance of him may still be seen in the figure of 'John Bull', as exhibited in *Punch*.

In Harley's time the ladies, putting aside working or household blanket-gowns, were 'in pleasing cotton dresses, scarlet plaids and duffle-cloaks.'

Harley paid £20,000 in wages annually to his winders and weavers of cotton yarn – around 600 people in total – besides large outlays on buildings, plant and labourers.

In 1812 he was one of the merchants who created the Glasgow East India Association which along with Liverpool and other cities successfully secured free trade with India and China. He sold across the United Kingdom and some of his products were exported to the Low Countries, the Caribbean and the USA where that country's textile manufacturing was still in its infancy but would in time benefit from the arrival of industrialists, dyers and weavers from Scotland.

Schools and academies in Glasgow and elsewhere taught practical arithmetic, weights and measures, accounting and banking for those setting out to work in business. Textbooks also provided examples from commerce, with Harley's firm featuring in one textbook devised by 'James Morrison, Accomptant, Late Master of the Mercantile Academy, Glasgow' which sold across the country in the 1810s reaching three editions.

After his textile manufacturing ceased in 1816 Harley's business address was now Bath Street at the dairy and baths. After the sale of Willowbank in the 1820s, the business address continued as before and the family's town address became Cambridge Street.

A biographer adds in 1901:

His portly figure, his blithe and jovial face, his big heart and kindly ways, his busy brain and his tremendous energy, could not fail to give him a prominent place among his fellow-citizens at kirk or market, when our city was waking from its long sleep, and entering upon a course pf prosperity of which the most sanguine in that day but little dreamed.

1814 example from *The Compendium of Practical Arithmetic*

BILL of PARCELS is a Note of the Quantity and Cost of Goods sold, which is delivered to the Purchaser, by the Seller, along with the Goods.

Mr. James Hutchison, Glasgow, March 16th, 1814.

Bought of William Harley & Co.

		£	s	d
$\frac{7}{8}$	Cossae Muslin, 100 ps. each 28 Yards, at 13d.	£151	13	4
$\frac{4}{4}$	Grey Cambrics, 100 do. do. 24 Yards, at 16d.	160	0	0
$\frac{5}{4}$	Shawl cloths, 100 do. 100 dozen, at 18/6	92	10	0
		£304	3	4

At the New Year Sales, The Looking Glasgow, 1825.

Chapter 3

Schools for All

Punch & Judy Show on Glasgow Green, The Looking Glass, 1825.

Before expanding west over Blythswood most townfolk stayed around Glasgow's High Street and Trongate, with George Square's streets emerging, where William Harley lived before his marriage. The city's population was now 66,000 with more schools being required to add to the couple of burgh schools which taught on weekdays.

To help children and families who had no schooling, most having to work six and a half days a week, Harley opened two schools.

In the 1790s, before the police force was formed in 1800 – Britain's first – William Harley took his turn with fellow-citizens in patrolling the streets on night watches. His beat was in the Saltmarket and Briggait and in his diaries he notes the 'shoals of neglected children amidst scenes of depravity...... in this Billingsgate of Glasgow.' Sabbath schools started around the 1790s, becoming well established in the city

The Merchants Hall and Steeple, Bridgegate, near the Clyde, drawing by William Simpson.

and imparting moral instruction to children. William Harley assisted and his clerks kept note of the number of schools, scholars in each and books distributed.

Schooling in the Merchants Hall and Anderston

From 1797 to 1802 Harley superintended weekday evening and Sabbath schools in Bridgegate Street, with his clerk keeping the registers. For accommodation, and despite opposition, he got use of the garret of the Merchants Hall, the start of a new school for 400 pupils. The Dean of Guild gave permission for skylight windows to be installed, bringing light into the roof space. This was a children's church – in a style which the Glasgow Foundry Boys Society would develop – where a short address was given and portions of Scripture taught. When the first summer arrived the whole garret had to be given up as it was the storeroom of the town's street oil lamps now that winter had gone! The grand Merchants Hall itself became the home of Bridgegate School on the Sabbath.

However, many of the children and adults could not read. William Harley now hired four apartments in the building and, getting his own warpers and clerks for a small extra salary, two shillings and sixpence a week, to act as teachers, 100 boys and 100 girls were taught the art of reading from seven o'clock in the morning. Those on public work came in the evening from eight to ten. Two years later he records in his diaries: 'About four hundred children and adults were taught to read the Bible who did not even know their alphabet when they first attended the school.'

Around 1810 Harley opened another school and

owned the new building. This was in Anderston to help educate its many children. It was the third of four new day schools planned to open at the one time in Glasgow – one for each quarter, in the east at Calton (Green Street), in the south at Gorbals (Portugal Street) and west at Anderston (Argyle Street today), but the one for the northern district was not built because too much had been spent on the Anderston one.

These came under the Lancasterian Society principles using a small number of teachers helped

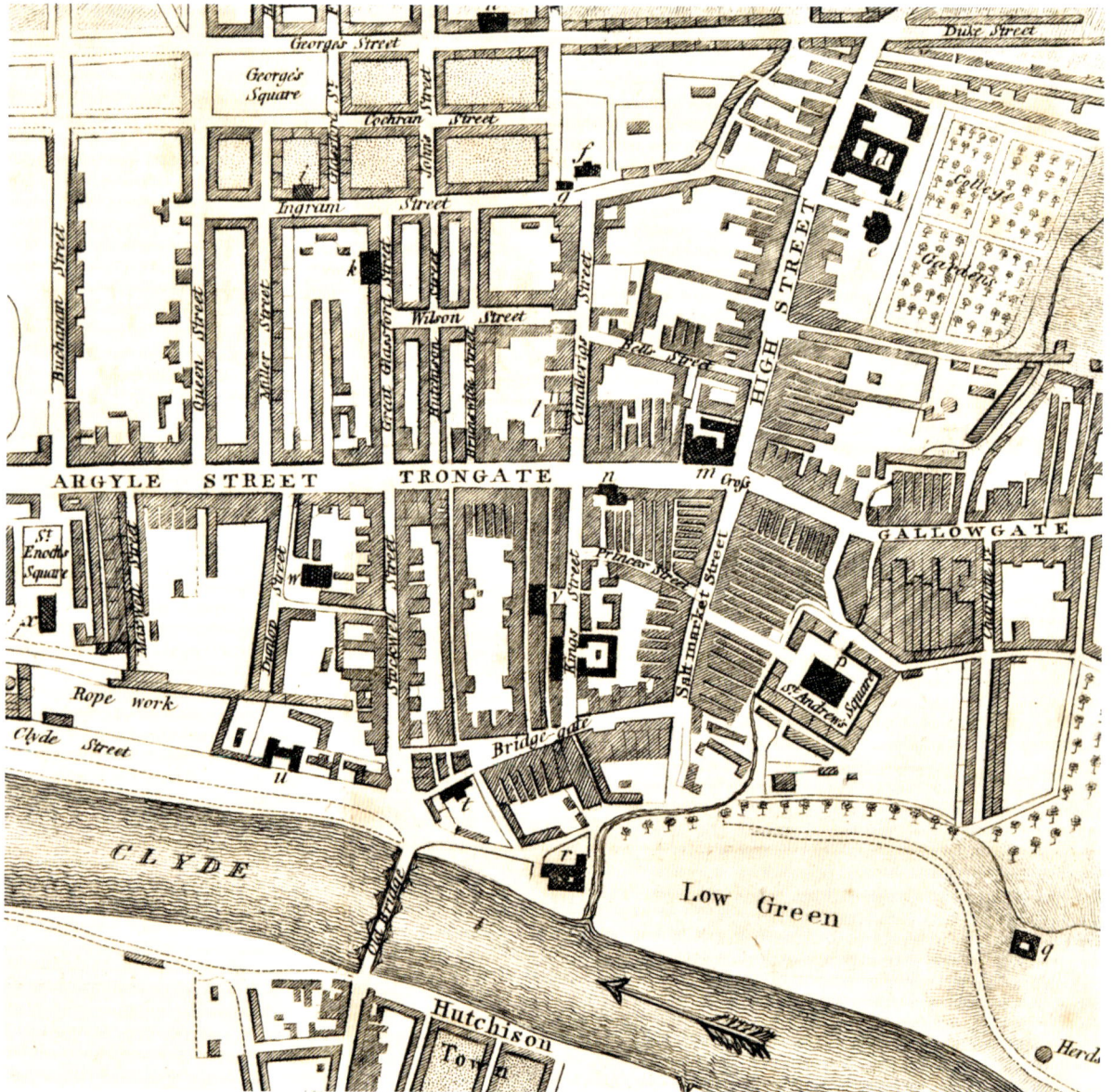

Congested areas around Glasgow Cross and Saltmarket Street, mapped in 1797.

by the older children, once taught, mentoring the young ones. The schools were 'for the purpose of Educating and Instructing Children of the lower classes of the community at a cheap rate – one penny to threepence a week – or for gratis, to those who could not afford a small fee.'

The society followed the lead of Joseph Lancaster, a Quaker in London, who started the first monitorial school around 1800 by superintending a new, non-sectarian, Free School in London chaired by a fellow Quaker, the merchant Patrick Colquhoun once of Kelvingrove House, now of

Site of the New British System of Education School, Anderston Walk, mapped in 1821.

London, who had founded Glasgow Chamber of Commerce.

It was the national secretary of the new Society, Joseph Fox, and now also a partner in David Dale and Robert Owen's New Lanark, who reflected in 1814 that Glasgow was the first city in the kingdom and its dominions to decide to build four Lancasterian schools at the one time; assisted in design and building by loans from the Royal Bank of Scotland. The new school fronting Anderston Walk stretching between Carrick Street and McAlpine Street – with its name *New British System of Education* emblazoned along the façade – had 320 pupils attending. It was a substantial academy with offices at the back and a playground along the front divided by a railing – one half for girls and one for boys. The main block was a large hall with a lofty ceiling. Every branch of education was taught by the two teachers helped by numerous monitors. Two of Harley's sons were educated here as were others of fellow merchants. It was converted to a granary after the school ran out of money.

Lancasterian schools opened in Edinburgh, Dundee, New Lanark and elsewhere. Most popular south of the border and overseas, and known as the British & Foreign Schools, the monitorial schools in Scotland later changed in favour of schools as pioneered by the Kirk in the eighteenth century but with more and better-trained teachers and a more mutual approach, thanks chiefly to the work of David Stow. He had started in Paisley as a draw boy to a weaver, moving to Glasgow in 1811 to work in the silk and cotton trade.

Systems ahead of their time

Others extending education in Glasgow included the eloquent minister Dr Thomas Chalmers and the printer and publisher William Collins in Candleriggs. David Stow, like Chalmers and Collins, was unimpressed by the claims of the Lancasterian system. He led two Sabbath schools in deprived areas. In the Drygate in 1828 he converted a large house and garden into a day school for 100 pupils and encouraged student teachers, male and female, to observe his new methods of learning by enjoyment. This was

The Normal School today in Cowcaddens, built 1837.

Jordanhill College of Education.

the start of his pioneering Training System of Education which would become known across the continents as the Glasgow System.

In 1837 at New City Road, Cowcaddens, David Stow opened the immense Normal School for the Training of Teachers, led and directed by him. This was open to all denominations and was the first institution built in the United Kingdom as a teacher training college. It was given to the Church of Scotland two years later. And he did the same again in 1845 for the new Free Church of Scotland, being the Free Church Training College, also in Cowcaddens. In the twentieth century their city successor was Jordanhill College of Education.

A year before his passing in 1830, William Harley published his scheme for compulsory schooling – he conceived when he superintended schools in the Briggait and anticipated the Lancastrian schools. It forms the closing appendix to his book titled *The Harleian Dairy System*. Compulsory schooling would be for all children across Glasgow, in all districts, and involve erecting buildings, engaging teachers and inspectors and having a rotating library. But he was 70 years ahead of his time. Compulsory schooling had to await its introduction by Act of Parliament in 1872, and compulsory attendance in 1880.

Chapter 4

Blythswood Pleasure Gardens

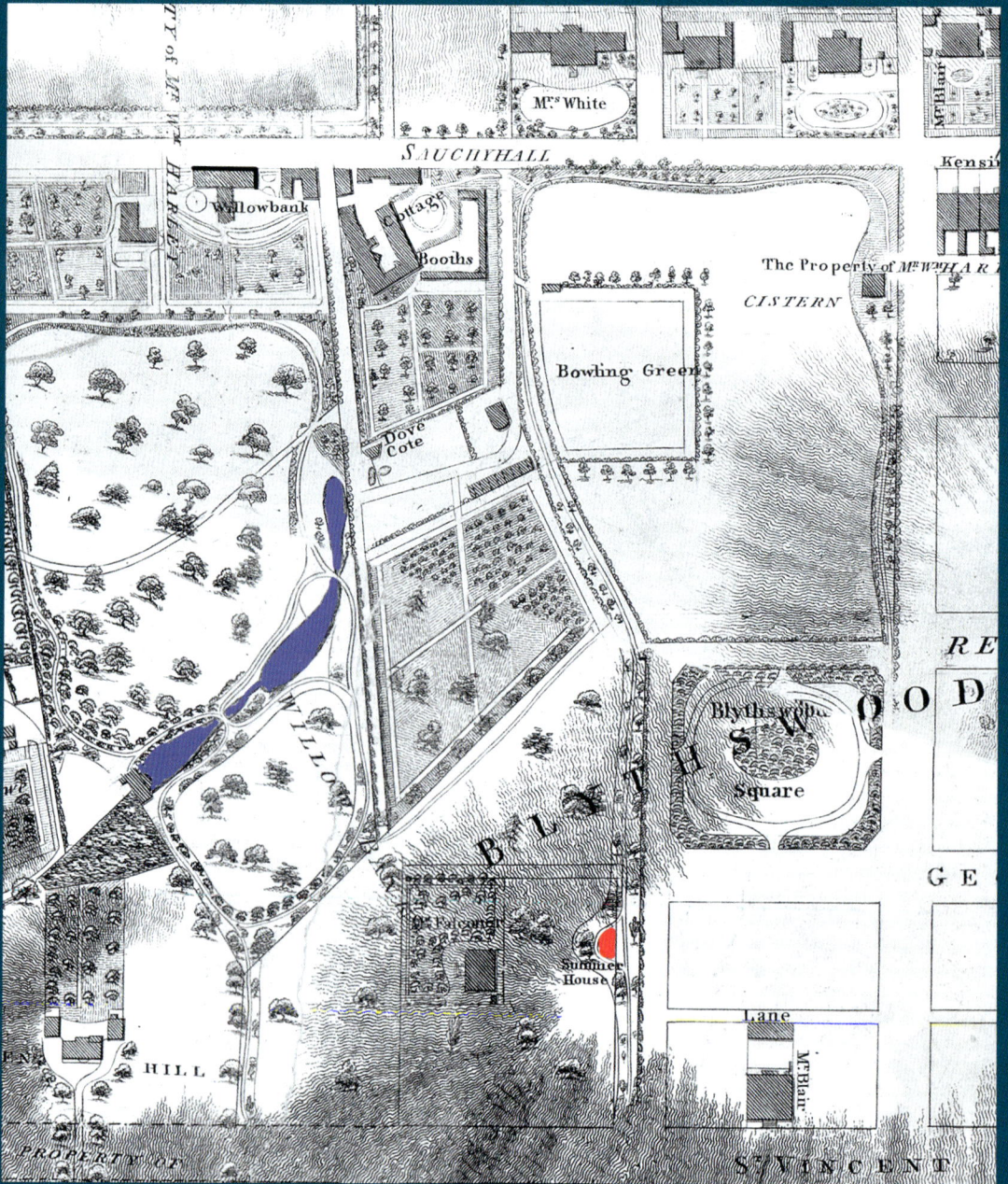

David Smith map of 1821 showing Willow Bank and its outbuildings next to Saughyhall road, with Harley's Pleasure Gardens and fruit groves extending south-west and south-east to St Vincent Street. The ornamental lakes are shown in blue and the Summer House in red.

William Harley became known as the Great Improver. He was full of ideas, often ahead of his time, and needed space.

Blythswood Hill

It was 1792 when army officer John Campbell, who was a Douglas, obtained his Act of Parliament to permit selling the inherited Lands of Blythswood 'to the great beauty and advantage of the town and the benefit of John Campbell and other heirs'. All 470 acres of open ground could now be sold stretching west from Buchanan Street to Kelvingrove and north up to Woodside and the future Great Western Road. Some properties already existed along the edges, mainly near the village of Anderston close to the Clyde, with its Delft-works, Verreville glass-works, brewery, textile mills and weaving. In 1800 his kinsman Colin Campbell advertised that he was ready 'to let all his lands near Glasgow on leases of ninety-nine years, except about 150 acres close to the town'. The ones close to the town were for sale. Land continued to be stated in Scotch acres, which are about one third larger than Imperial acres.

Lt.Col. John Campbell of Blythswood, caricature by John Kay.

The colourful panorama of Glasgow painted in the 1810s by John Knox, viewing north across the Clyde, shows some of the hills surrounding the city. In the close-up looking beyond St Enoch's kirk spire is seen the summer-house and viewing tower built by William

Springtime in Blythswood Square.

Panorama of Glasgow from the south-side of the Clyde, painting by John Knox, 1817.

Harley on the top of Blythswood Hill, and across the gully of the Sauchie haugh is Garnet Hill showing the new Observatory on its top. Through the haugh ran a quiet rutted road lined by sauchs (the Scots and Old English term for willow) and some rustic cottages. This was the Sauchie Haugh road, later to be known as Sauchiehall Street.

Willow Bank and Blythswood Gardens

Close to today's Blythswood Square, but many times larger, emerged the Blythswood Gardens and its mansion Willow Bank, the domestic centre of William Harley's ventures.

Successful in his textile business and newly married to Jane Laird, the ever-active William bought the 10 acres and new villa of Willow Bank in 1802 (just west of his future Blythswood Square). The family settled in Willow Bank with space for leisure gardens and vegetables and fruit, prompting ideas to

Dr. Thomas Garnett.

develop further. In 1804 he bought 35 acres of Blythswood from Campbell containing its Hill, equally known as Harley's Hill – down to Blythswood Holm at its lower level – and its northern summit which Harley named 'Garnett Hill' as a mark of his respect for Dr Thomas Garnett, one of the earliest professors of today's Strathclyde University. A mile to the north was the canal basin of Port Dundas, flourishing as Glasgow's harbour with its ships' masts piercing the skyline, and surrounded by its granary, distillery and mills.

He also bought 36 acres of grass parks and garden ground of Sight Hill farm, north of the new Royal Infirmary. It overlooked the city and the thirteen counties visible from its height 400 feet above the Clyde. And in 1810 he bought (from the banker and treasurer of the Observatory) the eighteenth century mansion of Enoch Bank, close to the future Renfield Street, with its narrow 4 acres angled northwards to its entrance from Sauchie Haugh. It was advertised then as 'lying within ten minutes' walk of the Cross of Glasgow. The house consists of 13 fine rooms, with light and dark closets. In the kitchen there is a remarkably fine well.' Enoch's Burn, next to Enoch Bank, had good running

Close-up in 1817 of the hills northwest of the city, with Harley's Summer-house and Viewing Tower on the first hill, left, and Garnethill Observatory on the second hill.

Fashions for June, The Looking Glass, 1825.

water, and the new houses in Buchanan Street also had access to it. It was a trouting stream with trees on its banks down to the Clyde.

Including Sight Hill farm, William Harley controlled 85 Scotch acres of land, which is around 43 hectares in today's money.

The Willow Bank House was newly built for Lawrence Phillips, a member of the Trades House of Glasgow, whose calico printworks was one of many in Anderston. Phillips was the first person to buy from the Campbells under the new Act of Parliament. The land surrounding the mansion

was improved by him, and on Garnet Hill he permitted the townsfolk to graze their cattle. He also sold ground to others for their villas on the future St George's Road. The springs at Willow Bank helped supply a reservoir further south for his calico works and some of the land was used by Phillips as a bleach-field for his textiles. When his business ceased he had to sell his properties, with Harley buying Willow Bank.

The house was 'fitted for the accommodation of a respectable family' with a dining room, drawing room, parlour and six bedrooms with fire-places, apart from in the garret. There was also a stable, with stalls for four horses, a gig-shed, two outhouses, a hot house 'with pine stove' and a green house. The property included a thatched cottage, several small houses and a starching-house. Here and over Blythswood William Harley improved and cultivated the largely barren land and raised fruits and vegetables for the city; his orchards contained 500 apple and pear trees and his garden grounds on Blythswood Hill contained about 5,000 gooseberry and currant bushes. He nurtured five acres of strawberry fields on the south-facing slopes of Garnet Hill across from Willow Bank. In many a household or club the discussion was lively 'across the walnuts and wine' about what Harley planned to do next.

The fashionable resort of the citizens
William Harley created pleasure gardens of great extent and beauty, with arbours, gravel walks and grass walks 'surrounding the fruit gardens, with flowers and ornamental shrubbery on each side' all bordered by fancy horn-beam and beech hedges; and a tea garden with its own shrubbery, circled by hawthorn hedging rising

to the summit of the hill. An observer writes 'he reclaimed and cultivated Garnet Hill, and grew there strawberries of a particularly fine flavour for the enjoyment of the visitors to his Blythswood gardens, while the cream to be consumed with these dainties came from a farm which he purchased at Sighthill'.

To his grounds he added a dovecot and ornamental ponds, with fountain, on the low levels fed by the springs, with Chinese bridges across. He opened the Blythswood Gardens for public amusement for a small entrance charge, 6d and 1/-, attracting visitors from the town, for healthy walks and picnics and to admire the views all around. Season tickets were available. A feature of the gardens, close to his planned Blythswood Square, was a summer house surmounted by a pagoda-shaped tower, thirty

feet high, commanding a magnificent view over the city, miles of the Clyde and the surrounding country-side. Also from this site, as Harley writes, 'I could witness by a telescopic view, the distant operation of my servants in the garden and farm, which was found to be of great advantage'.

He constructed a large bowling green in one part of the Blythswood Gardens – bowling having been popular in Glasgow since the seventeenth century. A smaller bowling green and ornamental pond were built at the east end of the new Bath Street, close to a drying green ahead of his planned public washhouse and baths. The arrival of an Observatory stimulated interest. The *Glasgow Herald* reported that 'the tea gardens were the fashionable resort of the citizens on Sundays and holidays'. A writer in 1849 recalls, 'It was the rural rendezvous of

Port Dundas on the Glasgow Canal, drawing by James Hopkirk, 1820s.

thousands of our citizens who regarded a visit to the gardens as a trip to the country, and in those days it really was so'.

The Harleys' house bordered Sauchiehall road between today's Douglas Street and Pitt Street. The road through the Sauchie Haugh was a minor one only 28 feet wide with green fields and no structures along its southern border – except for a notable wooden bothy on Harley's ground 'which did amazing duty as a huxter's shop, as a side post office. as a dispensing establishment for the supply of Airthrey Waters which were always kept in stock, and which were held in great repute by bilious West-enders after what they would call a "jolly night out"'.

In 1819 several proposals came forward for a colossal Wallace Monument to be built in the Glasgow area. One correspondent proposed in the *Glasgow Chronicle* that it should be sited on top of Harley's Hill, to be cast-iron 120 feet in height and within the limbs and torso of the hero there should be stairs, balconies and tearooms. One foot would be a water reservoir, the other stabling for visitors horses. 'The head lighted with gas, might be an observatory, a small rotunda theatre or concert and assembly room. His sword might serve as a thunder-rod'

By 1820 Blythswood Square was set out and the public were invited to see Harley's plans for the new houses. Once building upon Blythswood got well under way, the large bowling green moved towards the new Elmbank Street in 1835, adopting the name Willow Bank Bowling Club – also known as the Elmbank Bowling Green – with an annual subscription of one guinea. In the 1860s it was built over by an extension

Enoch Bank mansion house.

Willow Bank Bowling Club centenary badge.

to Glasgow Academy, and when the Academy moved to Kelvinbridge in 1879, Glasgow High School moved in. The High School continues today at Anniesland Cross. Willow Bank was the first bowling club in Scotland and continues today in Dowanhill.

To the south of the pleasure gardens, Blythswood Holm had 'fruit trees and bushes well watched in the autumn' and closer to the houses of Anderston there were kitchen gardens run by the villagers and nurseries for the more well-to-do.

Glasgow Botanic Gardens

The example of William Harley's horticulture and laying out of Blythswood Gardens, new roads and pathways, encouraged a fellow merchant Thomas Hopkirk to come forward with his idea. The erudite Hopkirk was a son of a wealthy Tobacco Lord. The family's country house and estate, Dalbeth, a few miles east of Glasgow Cross, was where he

Fashionable Promenade at the Botanic Gardens, The Looking Glass, 1825.

was growing a vast array of plant species and he became an authority on botanical sciences.

In 1817 Thomas Hopkirk founded the Royal Glasgow Botanic Institution which developed the eight-acre site he bought half a mile west of the Blythswood Gardens, at Sandyford across from what would become Royal Crescent. One of the shareholders was William Harley. Its gardens and glasshouses opened to subscribers, and to the public paying an entry charge. Hopkirk's head gardener Stewart Murray arranged its design and curated its thousands of plants, which were mostly from Dalbeth.

Harley's Blythswood Gardens and Hopkirk's Botanic Gardens were about the same size. In the 1840s the Botanic Gardens moved to their larger, current site off Great Western Road. As a landscape architect, Murray helped design Glasgow's classical Necropolis, opening in the 1830s, and he designed other cemetery parks including Sighthill Garden Cemetery which opened in 1840 and was developed as the Père Lachaise of Glasgow. The same Sighthill once farmed by William Harley.

Thomas Hopkirk also pioneered lithography, founding a lithographic business in partnership with printer John Watson. Their innovations include the world's first comic – published each week under the name of *The Glasgow Looking Glass*, with illustrations by satirist William Heath, and becoming *The Northern Looking Glass* as its distribution widened. The lively coloured cartoons of 1825 and 1826 depicting life and scenes in Glasgow are still available today, some being in this book. Likewise a series of monochromes illustrating Glasgow was published by the Hopkirk family in the same decade.

Engineers and Masons
Starting at Willow Bank, and then Blythswood Hill, the most important suppliers to William Harley's ventures were the engineers led by the eminent James Cook of Tradeston (who became a co-investor) and the masons, notably the firm of Gavin Lindsay.

Thomas Hopkirk, portrait after Sir Henry Raeburn.

As well as laying out new roads and promoting new housing, being built by himself or by others, Harley started a string of new ventures – all being in addition to his main textile business. He provided the first supply of piped water to the city, the first swimming pools and public baths, the country's largest and most advanced dairy, and a bakehouse nearby.

Critical to much of this construction was **James Cook** – a Baillie of Gorbals, inventor, mechanical engineer, agricultural engineer, civil engineer, and along with Robert Napier he founded marine engineering. He was a trustee of the River Clyde and Harbour of Glasgow Committee.

James Cook was a machine maker in the Cook family's large cotton spinning mill in Gorbals. He branched out in 1785 as a blacksmith, millwright and engineer with a small workshop near St Enoch Square. Soon he moved back over the Clyde to Tradeston opening his extensive premises, known as Cook's Works, in Commerce Street. In the trade it was known as 'the College' from the fact that many of the best workmen and engineers got their training there. Cook was a founder member of the Royal Philosophical Society of Glasgow – 'for the Improvement of Science' – which continues today.

Once Henry Bell successfully demonstrated the *Comet* in 1812 sailing down the Clyde to Greenock, the first seagoing steamer to sail in Europe, James Cook was the first to design engines expressly for ships and built numerous marine engines in his lifetime. The city's statistician James Cleland writes in 1817:

In 1815 James Cook exhibited and explained the principles of the machinery, paddles etc of a Steam-Boat to their Royal and Imperial Highnesses, John and Louis, Archdukes of Austria, with a view to these illustrious strangers placing steam-vessels on some of the rivers of Germany. Mr Cook has since furnished the Austrian Government with plans and models. Since the period alluded to, Steam-Boats have been built at St Petersburg, and are now plying on some of the rivers in Russia.

He also invented steam engines to power vast sugar mills, these being exported to every continent, founding the new sugar mill industry and making Glasgow its world centre of production.

For Harley, James Cook provided equipment for his new ventures and his workforce helped lay out most of the new streets, sewers – devising their own cast iron pipes – and mews lanes ready ahead of the housebuilding to come. Soon there were over 1800 masons on the New Town of Blythswood working for numerous clients. But Harley and James Cook would discover they were thirty years ahead of their time.

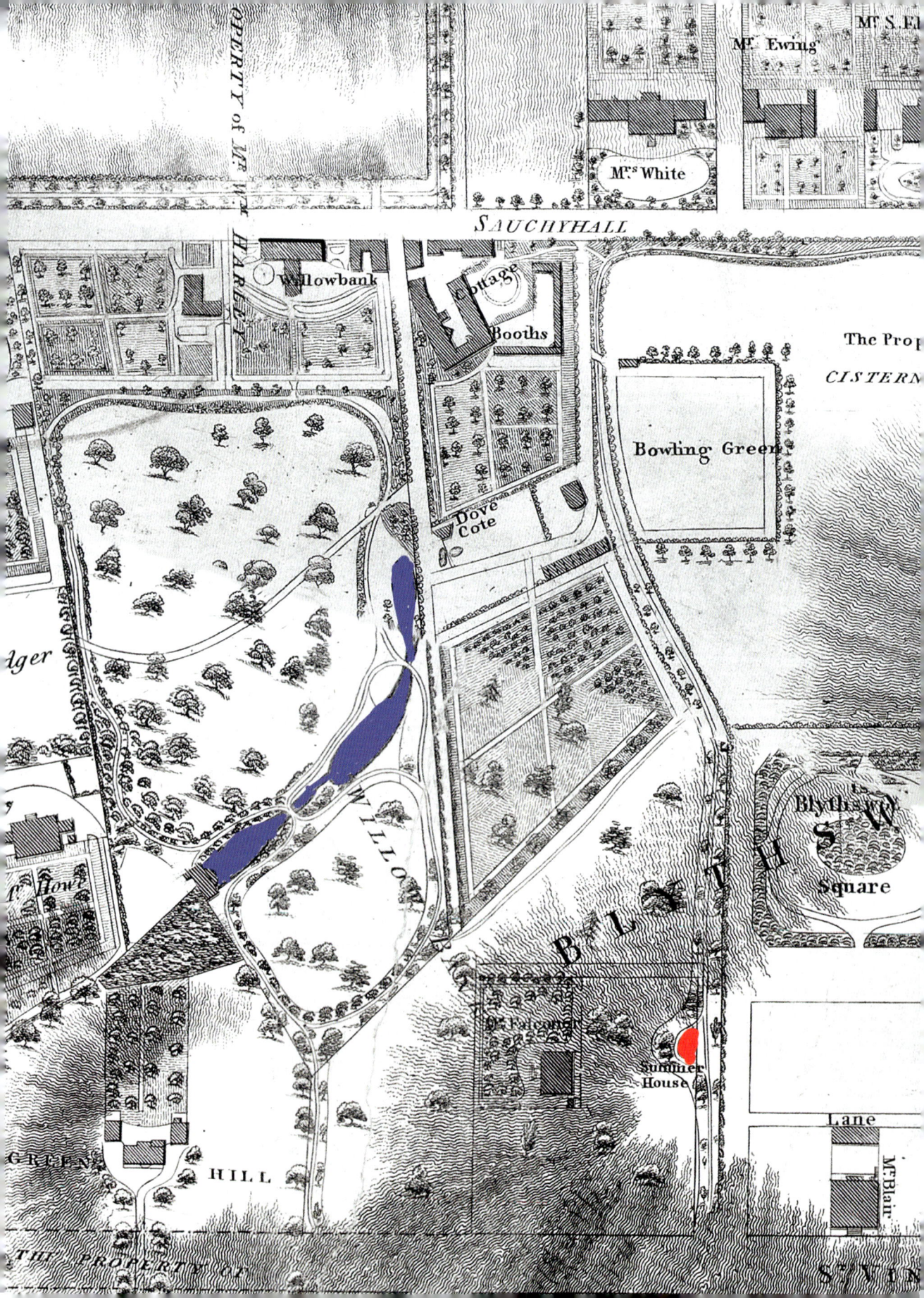

PROPERTY of M. W.

M. Ewing

M. S. E

M.s White

SAUCHYHALL

Willowbank

The Prop

Cottage

CISTERN

Booths

Bowling Green

Dove
Cote

HARLEY

WILLOW

Blyth SW
Square

BLYTH SW

dger

Howe

D. Falconer

Summer
House

Lane

M. Blair

GREEN

HILL

THE PROPERTY OF

ST W

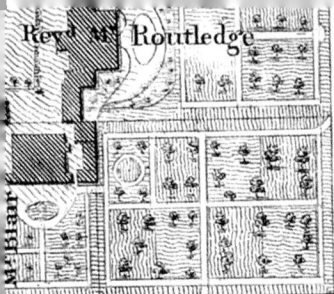

Rev.ᵈ M.ʳ Routledge

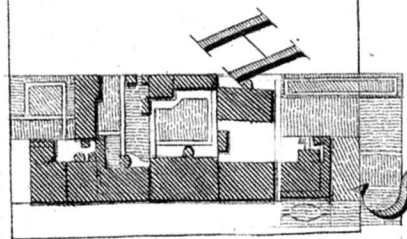

Windsor Place

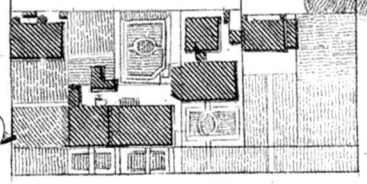

Wellington Place

ROAD
Kensington Place

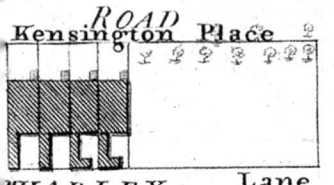

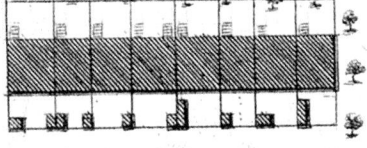

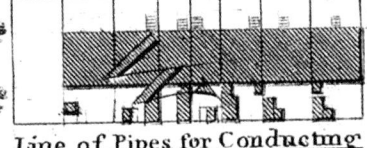

HARLEY Lane

Line of Pipes for Conducting Spring Wa

Bow
Gr

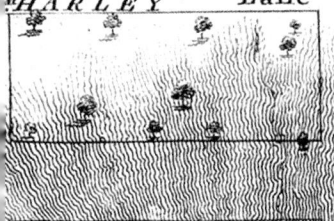

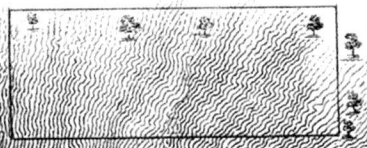

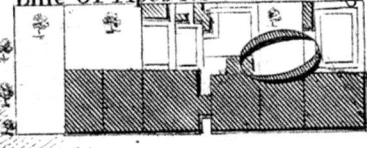

B A T H

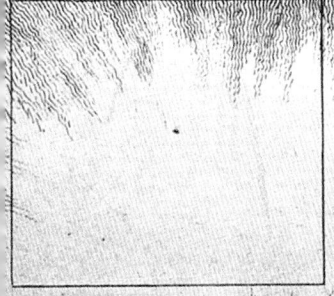

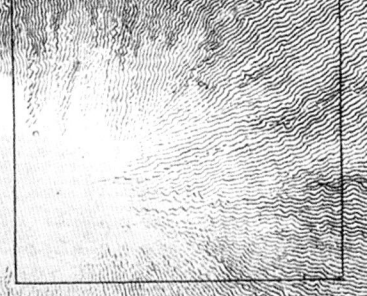

M.ʳ Macindæ

HOPE STREET

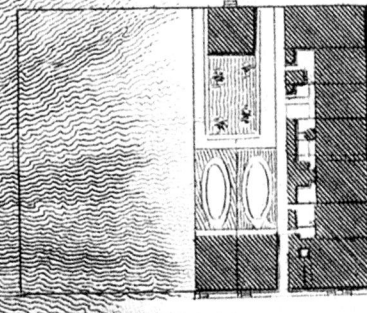

R E G E N T

D   H I L L

Lane

M.ʳ Bety

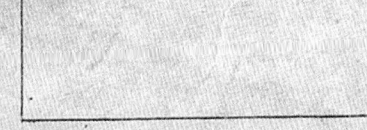

Moore

G E O R G E

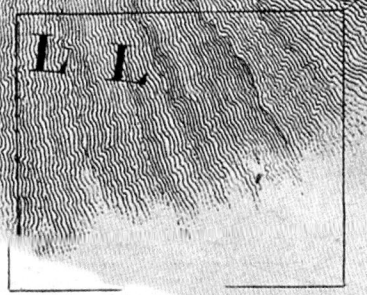

STREET

Lane

Lane

Lane

Lane

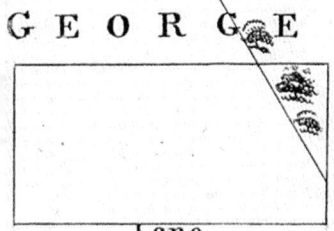

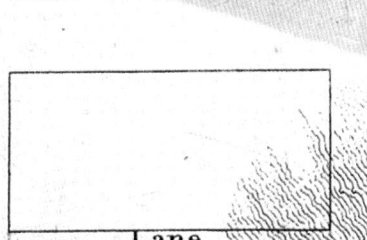

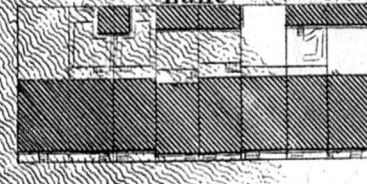

M.ʳ Debuøy

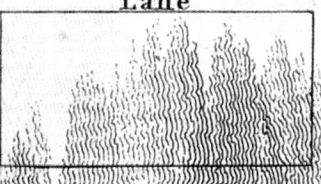

M.ʳ Muir

M.ʳ Graham

S T R E E T

Blythswood Place

Chapter 5

Promoting the Observatory

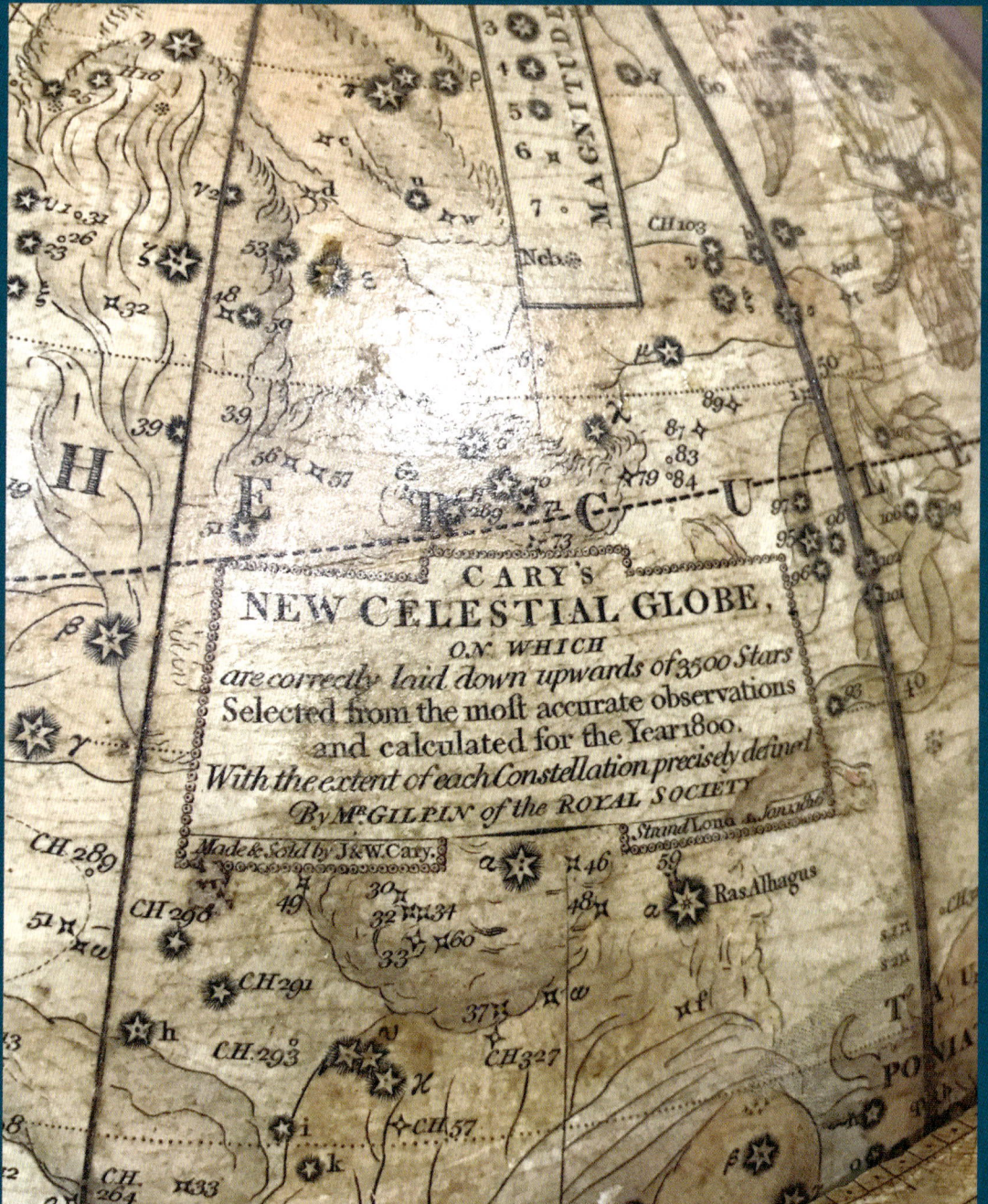

Cary's Celestial Globe manufactured in the 1810s.

Well established in his businesses and a supporter of the city's new Anderson's Institution – today's Strathclyde University – William Harley became a founding shareholder in 1809 of the Glasgow Society for Promoting Astronomical Science. This was the idea of the Institution's Professor of Chemistry and Natural Philosophy Dr Andrew Ure and would give 'the use of the Observatory and its Instruments and Books to the Professors and Students in Anderson's Institution.' Dr Ure was also a surgeon, distinguished writer and publisher, inventor and a promoter of free trade.

A large steading of land on Garnet Hill, suitable for the new Observatory and Camera Obscura, was bought from Harley and instruments were sought out. Dr Ure visited Largs, meeting fellow-astronomer Colonel Thomas Brisbane in his mansion Brisbane House who kindly gave advice as to what instruments to buy and at what price. Brisbane also inspected the new site. The Society described Col Brisbane (later General, and first Governor of New South Wales) as 'a distinguished Cultivator of the science of Astronomy.' Brisbane built his first observatory in 1808 on his estate in Largs. He became the first patron of science in Australia, including commissioning its first properly equipped observatory – with the whole of the southern skies to study.

Dr John Herschel, whose advanced reflecting telescopes would be used, also advised on the layout of the Observatory and frequently visited Glasgow. As the instruments were being commissioned and building work planned, the society took up Harley's offer to showcase what was to come. He was thanked 'for his liberality in offering the use of his Summer-House on Blythswood Hill as an Observatory until the new building opened on Garnet Hill.' On the day of laying its foundation stone in May 1810 the society's President, Rev Dr John Lockhart of College Church, led divine service in the newly opened St George's Church in St George's Place (the future Nelson Mandela Place) after which subscribers and families processed up to the site entered from Hill Street, watched by many spectators.

Dr Andrew Ure.

Sir Thomas Brisbane, portrait by F. Schenck.

Dr John Herschel, portrait by H.W. Pickersgill.

Hans C. Escher, engraving from a portrait by Martin Esslinger.

Garnethill Observatory and Camera Obscura, drawing by James Hopkirk, 1827.
Overleaf: David Smith map of 1821 showing Glasgow Astronomical Observatory, at the top of Garnethill, entered from Hill Street.

Revolving cupola and fine equipment

Designed in a neo-Egyptian style by Scots architect Thomas Webster – who designed the Royal Institution of Great Britain in London – the large Observatory had a revolving cupola and ranges of fine equipment for surveying and measurement including two Herschel telescopes. The larger one was 14 feet long with a 14-inch diameter and was the strongest in the kingdom apart from the one at the Herschel family home. The Camera Obscura was open to the paying public as was an exhibition area for amusement and education. The library of maps, charts, globes by John Cary, and treatises was next to the subscribers' club-room. The building contained a house for the superintendent, the first being Dr Ure. At a dinner in the city the Society presented Dr Herschel with silver-plate for his services in supporting the new venture. Herschel gave several lectures at the Observatory and in later years his son Alexander became a professor at Anderson's Institution.

A View from Switzerland

In 1814 a Swiss engineer and cotton merchant Hans C. Escher travelled round Britain studying its towns and trades. His three main towns were London, Manchester and Glasgow. After visiting Port Dundas and its ships in the canal basin, its granary and distillery – one of the largest of twelve distilleries opening in Glasgow by the 1820s – 'some charming houses built with beautiful local sandstone, surrounded by pleasant groups of trees' and 'numerous large foundries, chemical works and spinning mills of six or seven floors' he made his way down to Mr Harley's establishments in Bath Street, and the next day to the Garnethill Observatory.

He wrote much in his diary in September including:

> The owner of the baths is an enterprising and wealthy man because – in addition to the baths – he owns an exceptionally well operated dairy. We went to visit the fine Observatory which has recently been built here and saw a wonderful collection of instruments ………

> Above all I enjoyed the wonderful view which is better than any that I have seen so far. To the left lay Glasgow in a slight mist and to the right lay the valley of the Clyde. I could see the [High Church] Tower of Paisley, the hills crowned with wonderful groups of trees, the soft green meadows, the reapers in the cornfields. And beyond lay the hills of Dumbarton, Ben Lomond and the Highlands.

> Never before have I seen such a wonderful pattern of form and colour. Never before have I seen such architectural beauty in so fine a natural setting. There is a marvellous contrast in style and form between the 700-year old Gothic cathedral, the huge modern textile factories, the clean elegant public buildings, the mansions of the rich merchants, and the straw covered cottages of the poor muslin weavers. In no country in the world – and only in a few English towns – could one see such extra-ordinary contrasts.

> Nowhere on the Continent does one find – as one finds in Glasgow – buildings that are so functional in character.

But funds to operate the Observatory slowly ran out. It was offered to Glasgow University in the High Street, whose own observatory had ceased, but they had no money either. The contents were sold and the building was replaced by housing in the 1830s. The larger Herschel telescope was re-sited in the South African Observatory in Cape Town, where it is now on display in its museum.

GARNET HILL

Water Compy.

Hill

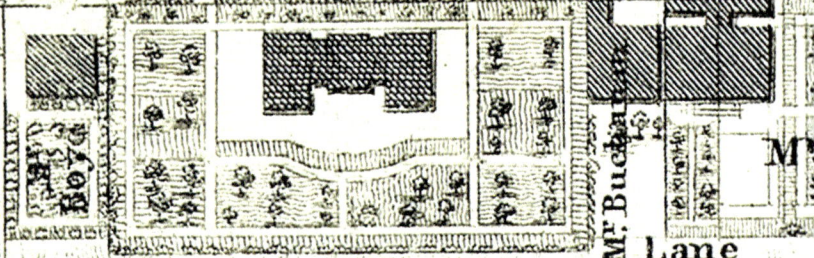

Mr Buchan St

Lane

Mr

Glasgow Astronomical
Observatory

Thistle

GARNET

PROPERTY of Mr Wm HARLEY

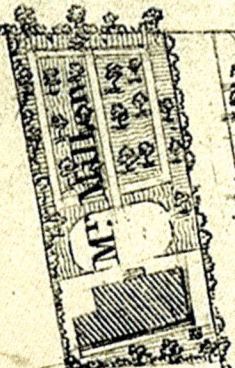

Mr.
RODGER

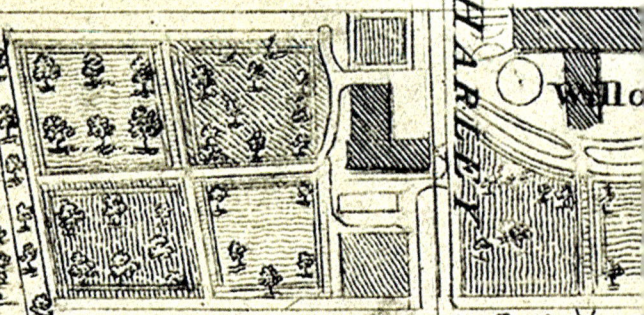

Well

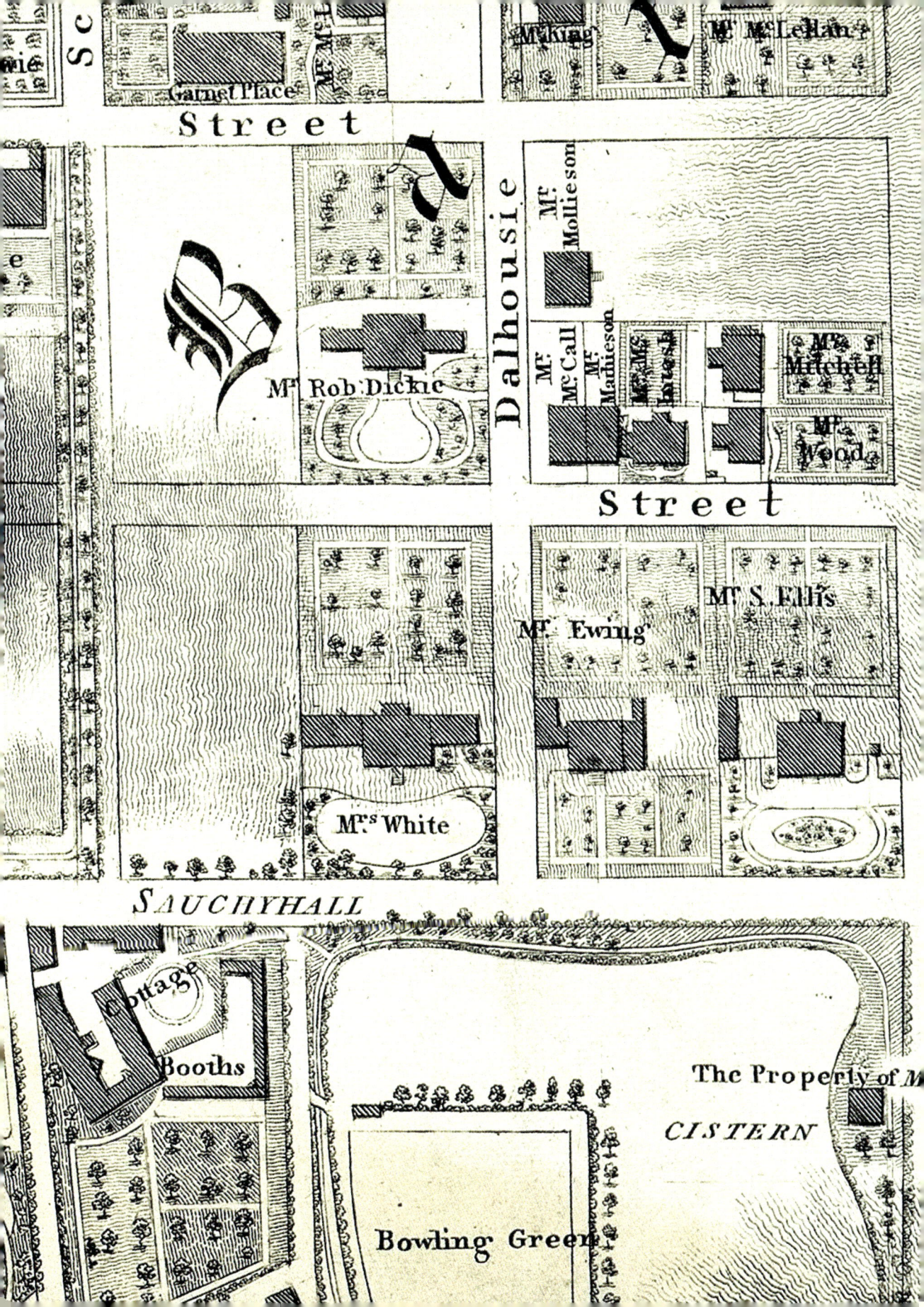

Sc

Street

Garnet Place

Mr King

M^r McLellan

Dalhousie

Mr Mollieson

M^r McCall

Mr Mathieson

M^{rs} McIntosh

Mrs Mitchell

Mr Wood

Mr Rob: Dickie

Street

Mr S. Ellis

Mr Ewing

Mrs White

SAUCHYHALL

Cottage

Booths

The Property of M

CISTERN

Bowling Green

Chapter 6

Harley's Water

Bath Street at the corner of West Nile Street, site of Harley's Establishment stretching to Renfield Street and Sauchiehall Street.

'The proprietor of the Springs at Willow Bank has resolved to bring the water to Glasgow in lead pipes, the cistern to be at the head of Nile Street, where a fountain will be opened for sale' – reported the *Glasgow Herald* early in the 1800s.

In Glasgow there were about thirty public hand-pump water wells, many undependable and some downright dangerous. More wells were added as the population soared. They were built of dressed stone from 10 feet to 40 feet in depth and protected by gates and lids. At the same time, some mansions had their own garden well.

All day long queues at wells would snake forward to obtain water for the chores, all very sociable unless a queue-jumper was spotted. At the main wells such as the West Port in the Trongate many servant girls with their hair neatly bound up in tresses with tortoise shell combs, and older ladies wearing mutches, were Highland and a great Gaelic babel of gossip would arise, all welcoming a break from other duties. They would each have two stoups, long wooden vessels with a cross bar at the top for a handle, with the owner's initials painted in bright colour, and

Glasgow Green, with a queue of maids waiting to draw water at Arn's Well, and porters nearby, engraving by Joseph Swan, 1820s.

sit on one stoup while the head of the queue was busy filling theirs. All would move up each time with a great clattering. The bevy of city porters helped carry the heavy full stoups over distances. The main High Street well was always queued by wives and weans, often with pitchers and wallie dishes instead of the aristocratic stoup.

Consuming water from a well, and likewise milk if available from a cow in a back yard, was a risk. Many people drank low beer instead. Numerous households started their morning with porridge and low beer.

Pure piped water

With his strong flow of spring water William Harley started more businesses to the benefit of fellow citizens. In his circulars he declared the purity of the water adding that it 'is better for many purposes than even Arn's Well' on Glasgow Green, which was then thought of as the acme of purity, especially for masking tea. He provided piped Willow Bank water to his houses being built and made it available to others in place of water from wells.

The fresh water came from new deep wells he built at the springs and was enclosed by pipes leading directly to a nearby metal tank reservoir, surmounted by a dolphin weather-vane, at the eastern edge of Willow Bank. At first, in 1804, he started to send filled square water cisterns, two at a time on elegant pony carts and four at a time on four-wheel spring carriages along the Sauchiehall road but this was often soggy and impassable with the rainwater flowing off Garnet Hill.

Very promptly a pipeline was installed along what is today's Sauchiehall Street Lane further east to an immense cistern at West Nile Street fitted with a fountain tap and another dolphin sign. The water was now sold there and in the deliveries throughout the city, on both sides of the river. An observer of the times records 'that two of these vehicles were of such enormous proportions that the houses shook as they passed, so that the Magistrates afterwards interdicted their movements'!

On this site William Harley later opened and operated his Willow Bank Baths, Scotland's first public indoor swimming pools.

In a circular Harley states:

> It is expected the springs will afford a sufficient supply all the year round but in the event of a scarcity a preference will be given to customers.

And he continues by taking time to advertise his building schemes:

> Two rows of houses are expected to be built shortly at Sauchiehall Road and that the top of Blythswood Hill has been laid out for building. It is not expected the ground will sell at present, but those who wish for a town and country residence may have an opportunity of examining the plan and be prepared to purchase when the times and price of timber are more favourable for building.

Napoleon had blockaded any trade with Britain, including stopping all timber from the Baltic.

Britain, particularly led by Pollok, Gilmour & Company of Glasgow, would now switch to sourcing and developing timber from Canada.

He adds a watery footnote:

> Stone or earthen pitchers should be used, as vessels of wood or iron give the water a bad taste. If one or more families take a cask for washing they will have it one third cheaper – say, three measures for a penny.

The standard price was a penny a gang or ½d a stoup.

'Willow Bank water, Sir, is softer than Clyde water, Sir'

Harley was advised to double his charges because of the superior quality but he chose to keep it the same price as the burgh charged for Clyde river-water. From his sales he made some £4,000 a year – an immense sum then. The daily luxury of having his pure water in cisterns being sent to each district morning and evening at set hours, heralded by a hand bell, was such that the people waiting were anxious not to miss the delivery. Otherwise it was a 'lang drouth' to the Arn's Well. Harley's advertising slogan was – 'Willow Bank water, Sir, is softer than Clyde water, Sir.' Each year on the King's Birthday Holiday and other special occasions he took out a procession of his twelve water coaches through the streets, the coachmen dressed in their fine livery.

William Harley strongly advocated that the city's sewage and waste which all reached the Clyde should be intercepted and collected at the river outlets to be converted into useful manure.

Loch Katrine.

Sewage treatment works only came into service in Glasgow around 1900.

Success in his water business stimulated others. From 1807 two companies started pumping and filtering water as best as could be achieved from the Clyde, at Dalmarnock in the east and then Cranstonhill in the west. They later merged and became Glasgow Water. Harley was a shareholder in the Cranstonhill Water Company which built a tank reservoir on the top of Garnet Hill. Harley now advertised that his new houses were ready for sale. These and the ones he planned for Blythswood Square could have a choice of piped water, either Willow Bank Water or Glasgow Water.

For the southside of the city and neighbouring Govan and Pollokshaws the new Gorbals Gravitation Water Company, building its reservoirs near Barrhead, announced in 1845 that its charges would be kept low 'by avoiding the costs of any development on the northside of the Clyde and need for reservoirs 200 feet high to serve Blythswood and Garnethill.'

In 1859 the immense Loch Katrine works were completed and switched on, bringing pure Highland water from thirty-five miles away to the city, district by district. Blythswood and Garnethill were connected in 1860.

Chapter 7

Harley's Baths in Bath Street

Tollcross International Swimming Centre, Glasgow.

Tollcross International Swimming Centre at the front of Tollcross Park in the east of Glasgow is of Olympic standard and one of the top ten swimming pools in the United Kingdom. The city's and Scotland's first public indoor swimming baths started on Blythswood Hill in the 1800s in what is Bath Street. This was a wonderful novelty.

A wonderful novelty

William Harley already had pipework installed to West Nile Street and his large cistern reservoir there – topped with a metal dolphin weather vane – was filled with abundant fresh water from his springs at Willow Bank. But the new Glasgow Water Company was installing pipes to all streets making his cart deliveries unnecessary. What to do with the spring water?

Harley completed his 'elegant and commodious' Willow Bank swimming baths and public washhouse around 1809. They were soon joined on the same city block by his advanced Willow Bank Dairy, with byres holding 300 cows, and his Willow Bank Bakery making quality bread.

The huge site today is bounded by Bath Street, Renfield Street, Sauchiehall Street and West Nile Street. It contains shops, houses, hotel accommodation and offices including the stylish headquarter building at the corner of Renfield Street built for the successful Glasgow Corporation Tramways. Also the Mechanics Institute in Bath Street, and the Empire commercial complex in Sauchiehall Street on the site of the famed Empire Theatre, successor to the Gaiety Theatre and earlier Choral Union Hall from the 1860s.

In quasi-Roman fashion Harley erected cold baths for swimming and hot and tepid baths for relaxing. The buildings of Harley's Baths sat in landscaped and spacious tiered gardens with gravel paths and shrubbery, lined by beech hedging. Some of the people taking the baths expressed a wish 'to be provided with warm milk after bathing' and Harley made available a cow from his farm at Willow Bank, 'gratifying his customers with tankards of warm milk'. From that start he developed a major dairy business.

A steam engine provided power and hot water (and central heating) for all parts of the site with a branch off to the baths. It would have been designed and constructed by engineer James Cook.

The architect of the buildings may have been the firm of Cleland & Jack who had built some of the houses in the first New Town and also manufactured furniture. They were the builders of the new Theatre Royal in Queen Street in 1805.

Around the time of Harley's baths being built James Cleland designed Bath Villa in Ardrossan which opened as a Tontine guest house with sitting baths, but no plunge baths. This was part of the Earl of Eglinton's plans for a seaside resort. Ardrossan town and harbour were being built to an elegant plan as the sea entrance to the planned Glasgow to Ardrossan canal. Cleland & Jack were to be the first to build houses in Harley's new Bath Street.

Advertising and ticketing

Harley describes his new venture: 'Warm and cold water flows into the baths. The warm water flows through a square tin vessel (pipe)

VICTORIA BATHS,

106 WEST NILE STREET, GLASGOW.

OPEN EVERY LAWFUL DAY FROM SEVEN O'CLOCK MORNING
TILL TEN O'CLOCK EVENING.

IN this Extensive, Complete, and Elegant Establishment, HOT, COLD, PLUNGE, SALT, SHOWER, DOUCHE, SITZ, VAPOUR, and MEDICATED VAPOUR BATHS, are in constant readiness.
A separate suite of BATHS and a Female Attendant for Ladies.
Charges for all kinds of Baths are on the most moderate scale.
. The Public are respectfully invited to inspect the Establishment, which, for Cleanliness and Comfort, will be found to equal any in the Kingdom.

Advertisement for the Victoria Baths in the 1850s.

and in doing so heats the vessel so that it can be used as a towel-dryer. The entrance avenues are formed with shrubberies and for the Ladies Baths are quite distinct from those leading to the Gentlemen's Baths. The Baths have all dressing-rooms attached to them and are provided with every suitable convenience.' Harley's advertising continues: 'When the weather is warm, they will be emptied two or three times a week, or oftener if thought necessary.' Swiss observer Hans Escher wrote in 1814: 'I thought the baths in Paris were much cleaner!'

There were seven main baths for ladies and children and seven for men, with the cold plunge bath for Gents being 57 feet by 30 feet and 4 feet 6 inches deep. The Ladies' plunge bath was 20 ft by 12 ft by 3 ft 6 inches deep, and for boys 12 ft by 10 ft by 2 ft 9 inches deep, and for girls 12 ft by 10 ft by 2ft 6 inches deep (girls being shorter).

Apart from three shower baths which were for washing, the baths included five stretching baths (one being made of marble, two Arbroath (paving) stone, and one deal/pine) and three chair or reclining baths (of Arbroath stone). All partially sunk in the floor. These bathrooms measured about 8 feet wide by 8 feet long; their

adjoining dressing rooms each having a fire. All were open from 6am to 9pm.

In the garden a half-moon shaped saloon or waiting-room 'decorated with many flowers' was supplied with London and Glasgow newspapers. 'Here one rings for the attendant and makes arrangements for a bath.' In this coffee room at the baths William Harley displayed elevations and plans of the houses he was building for sale.

Adjoining the baths, on the western side, was a very large public wash-house, with a drying green. He enlarged the washing-house 'with more conveniences which will enable Washers to do more work in a given time.' Nearby was another bowling green, similar to the one in his pleasure gardens, and an ornamental pond. On the eastern side at West Nile Street was the vast water cistern and the bath-keeper's house.

A complicated pricing covered all variations of Hot or Tepid or Cold small swimming baths, showers, and chair and stretching baths. Daily tickets could be bought in multiples of a dozen and were transferable e.g. 'Two of the Cold Bath tickets are taken for a Warm Stone Bath, and three for a Marble or Chair Bath.' For Cold bath swimming a single ticket was one shilling. Season tickets ranged up to 2 guineas a year.

From the mid-1830s onwards other bath establishments opened in the city being hot, cold or vapour baths 'for comfort and health benefit.' One also offered a swimming pool and was a replacement for Harley's Baths. Designed by architect James Smith of Blythswood Square, this was the elegant Victoria Public Baths opening in 1837 across at 106/110 West Nile Street. The new Bath Hotel in Bath Street recommended its patrons to it. Later in the century the Victoria Baths became the Accountants Hall of the Institute of Chartered Accountants and in the twentieth century was the headquarters of whisky firm Robertson & Baxter (now known as Edrington). Its sandstoned façade with the scroll doorway remains in place in West Nile Street. When the interior was demolished recently the baths' sloping floor was still in the basement.

From 1850 to the 1880s at least one swimming club also used the river Clyde at Glasgow Green with competitions over lengths of up to one mile, for a range of prize silver cups. Five large indoor swimming baths opened in the city, all being membership clubs. Two of them continue today – the Arlington Baths near Charing Cross founded in 1870 and which is now the oldest member-owned and run baths club in the world; and the Western Baths near Byres Road which opened in 1876. The first indoor swimming baths created by the town council opened in 1878 next to Glasgow Green. By 1914 there were over one hundred swimming clubs in the city.

View down West Nile Street today, with the façade of the Victoria Baths remaining in place.
Overleaf: Layout of Willow Bank Baths, with separate entrance gates and paths for Ladies and for Gentlemen from Nile Street at Bath Street, 1808. Ladies and children enter via the south path, while gentlemen enter via the north-east path past the semi-circular coffee house.

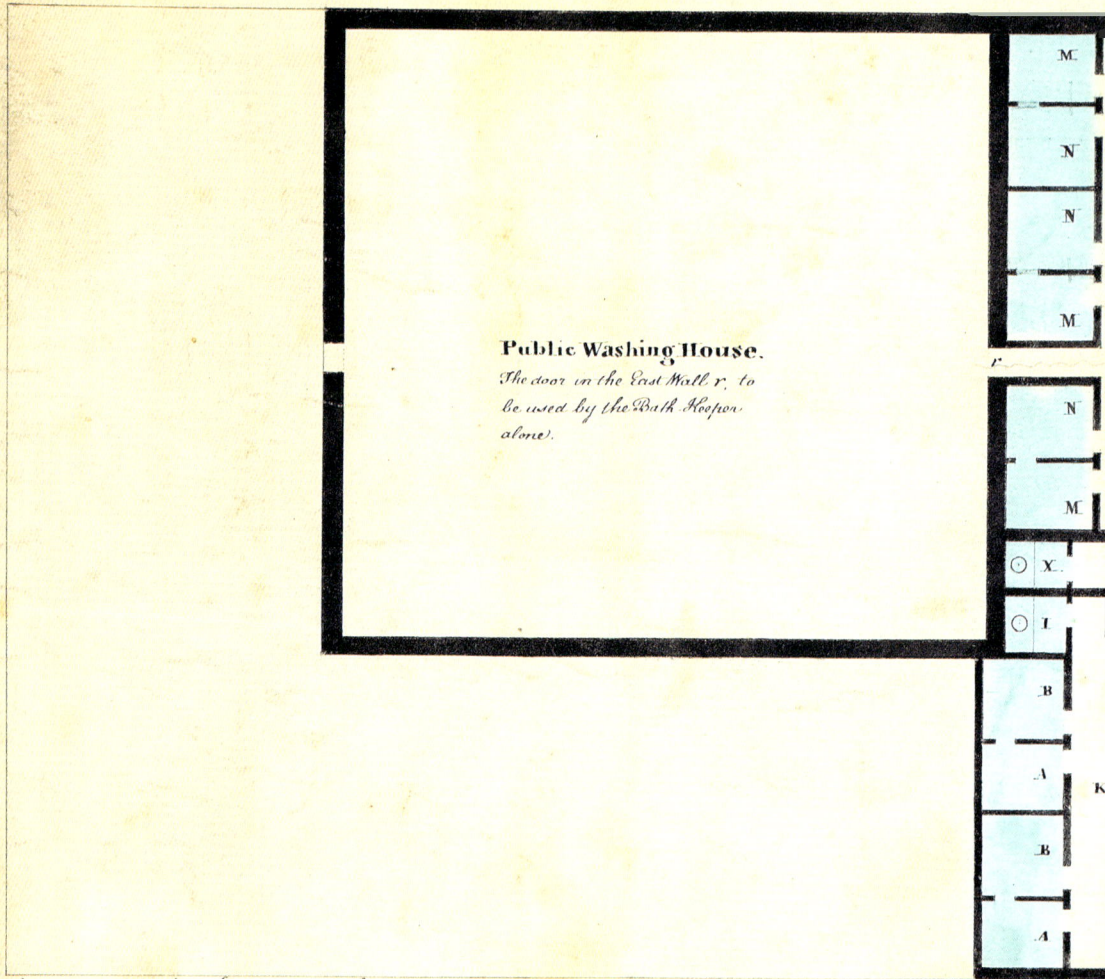

Public Washing House.

*The door in the East Wall r, to
be used by the Bath Keeper
alone.*

M.
N.
N.
M.
r
N.
M.
X.
I.
B
A
K
B
A

Explanation of the Baths for Ladies.

A.A, Private Hot Baths.

B.B, Dressing Rooms for the Private Hot Baths.

C, Public Cold Plunging Bath.

D.D, Private Cold Plunging Baths.

E, Dressing Room for the Public Cold Plunging Bath.

F.F, Dressing Rooms for the Private Cold Plunging Baths.

G, Public Cold Bath for Children.

H, Space for dressing Children.

I, Water-Closet.

K, Uncovered Passage.

L, Covered Passage.

Z, Shower-Bath.

Explanation of the Baths for Gentlemen.

M.M.M, Private Hot Baths.

N.N.N, Dressing Rooms for the Private Hot Baths.

O, Public Cold Plunging Bath.

P, Dressing Room for the Public Cold Plunging Bath.

Q.Q.Q, Private Cold Plunging Baths.

K.R.R.R, Dressing Rooms for the Private Cold Plunging Baths.

S.S, Shower-Baths.

T, Sitting Room for Bathers while waiting.

U, Cold Plunging Bath for Boys.

V, Space for dressing Boys.

W, Covered Passage.

X, Water-Closet.

Y, Uncovered Walk.

0   10   20   30   40   50   60   70   80   90 Feet

ng House.

T

Light Railway to convey things from the Bathhouse

Retaining Wall.

Y

S

U

P

G

W

Q

R

D

Q

R

C

D

Q

R

E

Q

R

S

Beech Hedge

Beech Hedge

Gate for the Gentlemen.

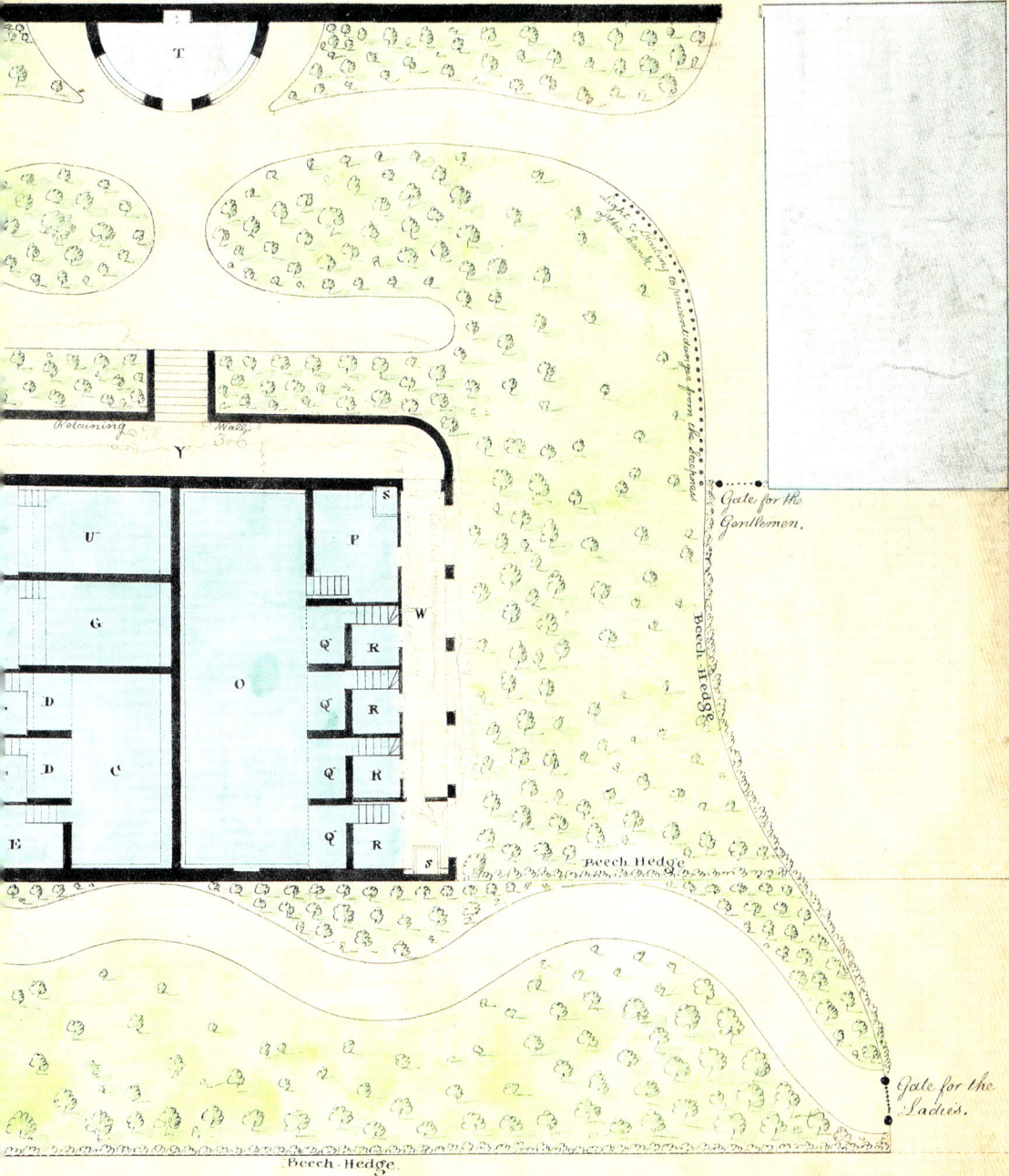

Baths, Bath Keepers House, and Cistern.

Gate for the Ladies.

Beech Hedge.

13th December 1808

Chapter 8

Harley's Byres and Willowbank Dairy

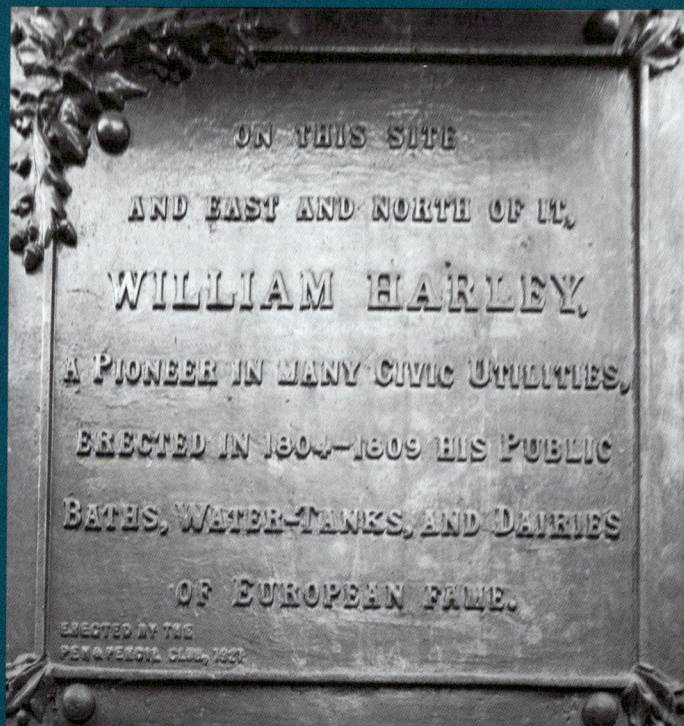

ON THIS SITE
AND EAST AND NORTH OF IT,
WILLIAM HARLEY,
A PIONEER IN MANY CIVIC UTILITIES,
ERECTED IN 1804–1809 HIS PUBLIC
BATHS, WATER-TANKS, AND DAIRIES
OF EUROPEAN FAME.
ERECTED BY THE
PEN & PENCIL CLUB, 1921.

Top: Bath Street panorama today on part of Harley's Establishment and its famed byres and dairy.
Bottom: Wall-plaque celebrating William Harley, placed on the corner of Renfield Street and Bath Street by the Pen & Pencil Club in 1921.

Early in his new public baths in Bath Street some customers asked for warm milk after bathing. William Harley sent along one of his cows from Willow Bank to be milked. Soon he had four next to the baths and in 1809 built a byre to hold 24.

William Harley now created the largest dairy in Scotland, recognised as the most advanced and hygienic in Britain. The new byres, better known as cow-houses, accommodated 300 cows. Its fame spread throughout Europe. He was the earliest promoter of modern clean dairying. Boston in America would be the next in 1859.

First to regulate a healthy milk supply

He was the first in Britain to set down rules to regulate a healthy milk supply. Pure and unadulterated. Cows' milk had been used mainly for making butter or cheese, which kept longer. For drinking milk, cottars historically used sheep or goats' milk. Some households kept their own cow but whether in villages and towns, or the greatly expanding cities, hygiene was not a primary concern. What cows ate and where they were, often in dirty surroundings,

Ayrshire cow, painting by William Albert Clark.

with no cow-cleaning nor clean handlers and containers, meant most folk avoided milk and its contamination. William Harley made milk safer and increased its demand. Milk now became part of daily food.

He offered both sweet full milk and, where cream had been removed for sale or churning, the watery leftover known as 'soor-milk,' also called skimmed milk. It was some fifty years later before Acts of Parliament started to require food hygiene.

Harley bought, and sometimes rented, cows from around the country. He trialled various types and decided to use one breed exclusively. These were brown and white Ayrshire cows – of Dutch origin – introduced from the 1760s onwards in Dunlop and Cunninghame, which would replace the small native black cows of Scotland. There were also some calves at the byres. Purely for visitors' interest, he added to the yard an East Indies' bull, normally kept at his Sighthill farm but imported originally by the Earl of Eglinton, and an East Indies cow and calf. There was also a large piggery of Berkshire and Chinese cross breeds.

Writes Harley: 'The milk is sent to the customers' houses, all over the town, twice a day, in labelled, locked vessels, so that the servants cannot, by any means, adulterate it (by adding water). These vessels are placed on spring carriages, and drawn by small ponies, to avert shaking as much as possible.'

The Willowbank staff also produced butter – once a fortnight – curds and cheese, with Harley extolling the virtues of buttermilk with cream and sugar: 'This is a dish worthy of being introduced

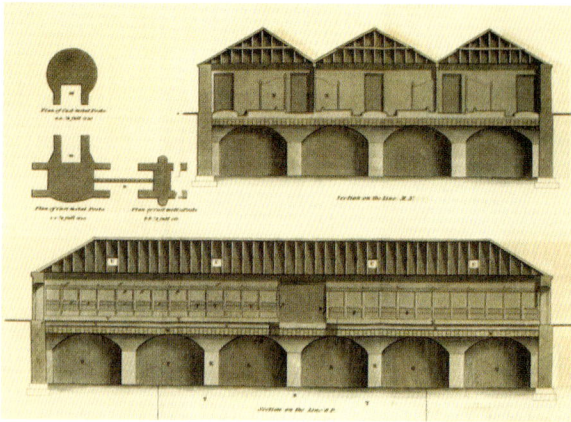

Cross-sections of a Cow House devised by William Harley, and engraved for his book published in 1829.

at the tables of the first circles.' William Harley soon supplied one third of all the milk in the city, earning him over £10,000 a year, a vast sum then. The normal price was sixpence per Scots pint, with skimmed milk much cheaper. A Scots pint was three times the volume of an English pint. Part-pints were also sold. Cream was three shillings a pint. Household bills were paid monthly. Of the city's 65 other registered cow-keepers who sold milk most had a couple of cows each; with only three or four having around 30 cows each.

By far the largest, Willowbank Dairy delivered 'Harley's Milk' throughout the town and suburbs, labelled 'New Milk' or 'Skimmed Milk' as appropriate. The ponies pulling the well-appointed carts, with harness and brass shining, had previously delivered Harley's spring water to all districts. The distributers rang their bell ahead of each street in their well-timed routes. 'Each customer knew, within a few minutes, the precise time when the milk would arrive.' The drivers were fined if they came back to Bath Street more than fifteen minutes later than scheduled!

Harley's Milk from cows as clean as cavalry horses

For its construction, Harley built over a ravine where coursed the Enoch Burn (later to be piped under the full length of West Nile Street and into the Clyde). On gently sloping ground he built several byres. The dry vaults of the bridge over the ravine included ice-houses for selling ice. Some of the wealthier house owners in the streets being developed also had ice-houses built in their basements. Harley also built a catacomb of cellars for storing porter ale. Cellars below the site and the mews lane were used for storing coal dross to power the furnace for the steam engine and boiler; and for storing hay, grains and vegetables, such as potatoes, turnips, carrots, cabbages and beans. 'The object of the Harleian Dairy was to fatten as well as to yield.'

Areas beneath the cow-houses were used for collecting the dung, used for his farmlands and fruit gardens – any excess being sold to other farmers. The soap suds from his adjoining public washhouse were added to the manure mix.

All the byres were well ventilated. One hundred cows at a time created a lot of heat! The last one built had thirty opening windows on its slated pavilion roofs, as well as windowed walls. Latterly, gas lighting was introduced to all the buildings.

The milk-office, kitchens and utensil stores were in the centre of the site. A counting office was at the gate and retail shops on site sold produce, vegetables and bacon. Completing the scene were stables for the ponies, cart-houses, a house for the manager and sleeping accommodation for several of the maids including the chief dairymaid, who was responsible for the milk-house, churn-room and dairy shop.

The steam engine provided hot water throughout and powered the machinery for hay threshing, corn bruising, potato and turnip slicing and for the churning vats. Ducted heating ensured a steady heat of around 62 degrees Fahrenheit, excluding the milk-house. The vegetables were steamed and cooled to form a mash for the cows, spectators calling it 'cow-tea.'

Byremen moved animals and supplies, and carted away dung. They, and the maids, washed out and sanded the stone floors twice a day; the men also whitewashing all the inside plastered walls once a week. Cow-maids cleaned and milked their cows, and prepared feed. Each maid milked from twelve to fifteen cows twice a day. Lactometers were used to ascertain the quality of the milk. Harley states: 'The milkers were generally women, their wages being only half that of men, and they were found to milk as well.'

Everything was measured and recorded. All utensils were washed and cleaned and scalded. The *Scots Magazine* reported: 'The floors are carefully washed twice a day and kept as clean as the lobby of a dwelling house. The whole cows are curried and brushed daily, and kept as clean as cavalry horses.'

In 1814 a deputation from the Highland Society came and studied his byres and dairy production with great attention to the hygiene of the cows, the buildings, the utensils and the milkers. The Society presented Harley with silver-plate suitably inscribed in recognition of his innovations. They added a request that he should write a book about his standards and methods to encourage others. A decade later he went on a continental tour during which he studied dairy husbandry in the Netherlands. He would add his assessment of it to his writings but it was June 1829 before he published his book *The Harleian Dairy System*, dedicating it to the Duchess of Leeds.

Charlotte, Duchess of Leeds, miniature on ivory, painted by Anne Mee.

Piggery pedigree

Next to the cowhouses was a large brick-built piggery housing fifteen styes, each with their own piped water supply similar to the cows, and straw bedding. A pillared canopy from the roof kept the area in front warm and dry. All the pigs were regularly curried and cleaned.

The Piggery, brick building housing fifteen styes.

Harley writes:

The piggery belonging to the Willowbank Establishment was kept chiefly for consuming the offals of the dairy, and the refuse of the gardens and farm, and also for turning the whole into manure. Every description of weeds and waste stuff was daily gathered and laid in front of the piggery, and a small quantity was thrown into its area every hour or two.

Most of the pigs were a cross breed of the Berkshire and Chinese. The Author paid £10 for a very large and handsome breeding Berkshire sow, and he got a Chinese boar from Lady Shaw Stewart of Ardgowan, which produced a breed of medium sized pigs. They were very handsome, quiet and good tempered; were easily fed, and when cut brought a high price for store pigs. They also sold readily for roasting.

Gentlemen or ladies who were accustomed to buy pigs for the dinner table, had them prepared for the cook and sent home from Willowbank. They willingly gave a higher price for pigs so obtained than for such as were exposed for sale in the market, as they were known to be cleaner fed and kept than by the common mode.

A tourist attraction

His unique byres and dairying became a tourist attraction. Local families and children were joined by dignitaries from home and overseas, including royalty from Russia and Austria, and other German princes and notables. Sir John Sinclair, advocate of land improvement and creator of the UK Board of Agriculture, was one of the visitors. Sinclair writes in his General Report of Scotland: 'If a plan and minute description of the Willowbank System were given, it could easily be adopted in every town in the kingdom.'

Visitors became so frequent that a raised viewing balcony was built outside the middle pavilion of one of the byres, with a curtain across the entrance. When the cow keeper raised the curtain by a pulley the spectators delighted in a panoramic view of the 100 cows and their attendants busily engaged, none distracted by the viewing. Copper-plate tickets of admission to view were printed depicting a woman milking a cow and groups of children drinking milk under the Glasgow Coat of Arms. Admission was a shilling. This created an annual income of over £200. Dignitaries and royalty were free guests! From Russia 'the Archdukes Nicholas and his brother Constantine drank a sup of milk out of a silver goblet.' On his visit the Grand Duke Michael did the same.

During 1829 Nicholas, now Tsar of Russia, requested William Harley to take over and improve the running of the Imperial Dairy in Russia, part of the 500-acre Alexander Park being designed by Scots architect Adam Menelaws. This is one of three parks next to Catherine Palace, summer residence of the Tsars, to the south

Sir John Sinclair, portrait after Sir Henry Raeburn.

A glimpse of Catherine Palace and parkland, near St Petersburg.
Overleaf: Milk Bar in Central Station, Glasgow, 1930s.

of St Petersburg. Unfortunately, Harley died at the start of his journey a few months later.

By the end of the nineteenth century dairying across the country reflected Harley's initiatives. Dairies and their retail shops now became big business including in the twentieth century such firms as Ross's Dairies, Scottish Co-operative Wholesale Society, East Kilbride Dairy Farmers, and originating from that town, Wiseman's Dairies, becoming the largest in Britain and now known as Müller.

A Government publication in 1946, following WWII, exhorted farmers across Scotland to construct new farm buildings, describing the achievements and standards of William Harley 130 years previously. In byres and dairy hygiene it states: 'Harley's ideas have stood the test of time and have been little improved upon since his day.'

In the 1930s the Scottish Milk Marketing Board, headquartered in Glasgow, and today known as First Milk, arose from earlier farmers' co-operatives. It dominated the milk trade and also promoted milk bars in many venues including Glasgow's Central Station.

Chapter 9

Harley's Willowbank Baking Company

In the 18th century it was in and around Bakers' Wynd at St Andrew's Square, off Saltmarket, where Glasgow's baxters (bakers) had their shops and ovens. It was noted by some that 'the bread being supplied was of an exceedingly poor quality and many were the complaints.' There had been urgent requests to William Harley to become a baker and supply the city with bread of a better quality. He resisted until 1815 when he agreed and added a bakehouse in Bath Street beside his dairy and the public baths. Bakehouses were also built in the basement.

Willowbank bread and bakery was sold in the city and sent 'to all the little towns on the Firth of Clyde to which the small fleet of steamers then navigating the river plied.' His property was just outside the city boundary and he did not have to pay the rates and 'ladle dues' that bakers in the town had to pay to the council each year. Demand for his bread was great and soon 20 tons of flour was consumed at the bakery each week for a total of six ovens. He claimed only Government Establishments for the army and navy produced more.

Willowbank baking included bread, rusks, bath biscuits (crackers), biscuits in variety, muffins, cookies and fancy loaves.

Bread, rusks and fancy loaves

The loaves were stamped with the initials of the firm, and the running number of the ovens. A quartern loaf was made from a quarter stone of flour and was almost two feet long.

Harley writes: 'Our flour is manufactured from the best wheat, without any mixture, from corn from all the best corn districts of Scotland.'

WILLOWBANK BAKING COMPANY
advertisement

The company's BREAD is of a much lighter texture and has more nutrition. The RUSKS will imbibe their bulk of Wine, Tea or any other liquid: – the experiment may be easily made. They also make FANCY LOAVES that will keep sweet for weeks and cut into very thin slices. Also GINGER BREAD of a superior quality, enriched with Orange Peel and the best of Seasonings.

The Quartern Loaves are all Superfine. By Act of Parliament they weigh 4lb 5 ½ ounces. The Half-Quartern are of three kinds; and the Small Bread of each kind in Twopenny Loaves. Biscuits are from 4d to 1s 6d per lb. Assorted biscuit selections are available from 10lb weight upwards in original Packages from the Company's Stores.

It was unadulterated by alum, used in varying amounts for whitening, and by potatoes which some competitors added to increase weight. Bakers from other towns tried to muscle in at a lower price, below the cost of wheat, and failed. In advertisements in 1820 Harley explains:

'The origin of the Willow Bank Baking Concern was by subscription from a number of the most respectable Bankers and Merchants in the City, whose object was *not to reduce the price* but to have *a superior article.*'

In his *Dictionary of Chemistry*, 1828, Dr Andrew Ure, now a consultant chemist in London, stated he had tested bread scientifically, concluding 'That alum is not necessary for giving bread its utmost beauty, sponginess, and agreeableness of taste, is undoubted, since the bread baked at the

The 19th century had books and rhymes about the Quartern Loaf.

The multiple branches of Glasgow bakeries reflected high quality and taste, photographed 1936.

Establishment of Mr Harley, at Glasgow, unites every quality of appearance with an absolute freedom from that acido-astringent drug.'

By the 1820s the Willow Bank Baking Company had branches in Port Glasgow, Greenock, Gourock, Inverkip and Belfast. From 1822 when his businesses and lands were put up for sale to repay his debts over developing Blythswood he relinquished all the ventures but became a co-partner of the Willowbank Bakery, where his son James was now general manager. In time,

the baking moved to new premises on the west side of Renfield Street.

Down in London, in November 1828, William Harley circulated 'a prospectus, to ascertain whether a sufficient number of subscribers can be obtained to indemnify him from the risk attendant upon such an undertaking in London' similar to the Glasgow baking establishment.

In Glasgow changes of ownership took place and as bakers and flour merchants Willowbank Baking moved to Cowcaddens from the 1850s until the 1880s.

Peacocks and pies

By the end of the 19th century Glasgow was the Second City of Empire and had bakeries to scale. The largest were Bilsland Brothers, William Beattie (who invented wrapped sliced bread), J & B Stevenson, United Co-operative Bakers, City Bakeries (the equivalent of J. Lyons & Co. in England), Macfarlane Lang biscuits, holders of the Royal Warrant, and likewise Royal Warrant holders Gray, Dunn finding fame with their Blue Riband biscuits. Others emerging included A.F.Reid (who also had a Cakery in Johannesburg), Currie's, Peacock's and James Craig, the King of Tearooms, who introduced 'French fancies' the equal of Paris.

Visitors to America often were told of their busy street vendors, boasting that in New York 'we have monkeys selling newspapers' to which a Glasgow reply was 'that's nothing, in Glasgow we have peacocks selling pies.'

MACFARLANE, LANG & Co., Ltd.

Victoria Biscuit Works, Glasgow.

Advertisement of biscuits by Macfarlane, Lang & Co., around 1900.

Chapter 10

The Campbells and Douglases of Blythswood

The Coat of Arms of Lord Blythswood. Douglas is superior to Campbell; the Douglas symbols include a man's heart, azure stars, red check, and oak tree.

Hailing from Glasgow, Argyll (Ardkinglas) and Lanarkshire (Douglas), the Campbell and Douglas kinsmen were adept at marrying wealthy daughters of the Tobacco Lords of Glasgow who controlled the tobacco trade between America and Europe.

Before that, Robert Douglas had married Isabel, daughter and heiress of the Elphinstones who long owned the Lands of Blythswood and Gorbals. As various estates passed on to brothers, sons, nephews or cousins the Campbells/Douglases adopted the surname necessary to qualify for the inheritance. Immediately to the north of Blythswood lay the Douglas family's estate of Mains upon which now stands Milngavie, and it was a Douglas who first assumed the estate of Blythswood and had to add Campbell to his surname.

By 1810 the Campbells were collecting almost £6,000 each year in feu-duties from around 150 feuars, never mind the one-off sales income from developers. Of this, some £1,000 a year in feu duty came from one person, William Harley, for central Blythswood and Garnethill.

The Campbells also collected around £3,300 a year from leasing out farms and quarries, especially in their county lands at Renfrew and Inchinnan. This all contrasts with an average wage at the time of under a £1 a week, and by 1900 approaching £2 a week. The annual property income of the Campbells grew tenfold before the end of the century.

Despite the oceans of wealth rolling into their bank accounts, from Harley and others, and holding early public posts and later directorships of companies the Campbells of Blythswood contributed little to the commonweal of Glasgow, with one exception. This was Archibald Campbell who became laird of Blythswood in 1868 and was later made the first Lord Blythswood. After his army career he was appointed Aide-de-camp to Queen Victoria. He became a Member of Parliament and later a scientist and colleague of Lord Kelvin.

The royal family, and siblings, cabinet ministers, and future monarchs of other countries were frequent guests at Blythswood House down-river

Mains House and estate, Dunbartonshire, one of the properties of the Douglas family.

Blythswood House and its setting where the river Clyde is joined by the river Cart.

Colonel Archibald Campbell, future 1st Lord Blythswood, as an officer in the Highland Brigade in the Crimean War.

Lord Blythswood in later life.

One of the rooms in Blythswood House.

at Renfrew over four generations. In 1894 a private 16-hole golf course was laid out in its grounds for family and visitors. A tennis court was added. The palatial mansion was demolished in 1935 and its grounds now contain Renfrew Golf Club.

Lord Blythswood created his own fully equipped science laboratory in Blythswood House to support his researches in astronomy, physics, radioactivity and cathode rays including the possibility of light-rays seeing through solid objects. For his scientific work and publications he was honoured by Glasgow University, the Institution of Shipbuilders and Engineers in Scotland and the Royal Society. Lord Blythswood completed his study and testing of cathode rays at the same time as Wilhelm Röntgen, but it was Röntgen who in December 1895 first published a paper on his discovery of X-rays.

At Glasgow's Royal Infirmary in early 1896 Blythswood assisted Dr John McIntyre and radiographer John Scott in achieving the first medical X-ray in Scotland and establishing the first radiology department in the world. McIntyre also produced the first x-ray films of limbs and organs moving in the human body.

One of Lord Blythswood's young brothers, Walter Douglas Campbell, assisted by their artist sister Helen, became the architect and builder of the vast and sculptured St Conan's Kirk on the banks of Loch Awe. Built for ease of use by the Douglas-Campbells and the local folk it was finally completed in 1930. A successor to the lairdship of Blythswood was Lord Blythswood's brother the Rev Sholto Douglas Campbell who became minister of St Silas' Episcopal Church, off Woodlands Road, Glasgow from 1887 onwards. The Blythswood title ended in 1940 with the death of twenty-one year old Philip Archibald Douglas Campbell in a car accident while returning to army camp in the black-out, when the remainder of their estates passed to his cousin Mrs Olive Douglas Methuen-Campbell of Innis Chonain, Loch Awe. The site of Blythswood House and its surrounding estate were later bought by the development company of hotel magnate Sir Reo Stakis.

Interior of St Conan's Kirk, Loch Awe.

Other descendants of the Douglases include Prime Minister Sir Alec Douglas-Home and Air Marshall Sholto Douglas (the future Lord Douglas of Kirtleside) who in addition to leadership in WWII became from 1946 supreme governor of the British Zone of occupied Germany with total control over all matters and people there.

On the east side of Blythswood Square.

Chapter 11

Planning it out

Bath Street at Adelaide Place, drawing by Sir Muirhead Bone.

It was agreed that Blythswood's New Town streets would have the same grid system as George Square, all streets at right angles to each other. The new streets had to be 60 feet wide and their pavements 9 feet wide before any building line.

Oddly enough West Regent Street appears to be narrower, perhaps adjusting to the boundaries of the thirty-five acres sold to William Harley in 1804. All of 'the houses to be built should not be of a greater height than three stories and a sunk story to the front.'

The Campbells' land agent was the distinguished surveyor William Kyle. He would keep record of all the developments and names of the new residents once houses were occupied. Kyle's expertise attracted clients and organisations in many counties, and his firm, later known as Kyle & Frew, survived into the 1960s.

As part of his land purchase it was agreed that Harley would be responsible for paying to the Campbells each year – for up to twenty years – the total worth of thirty-five acres of annual feu-duties. This large amount from Harley would reduce as and when he set out the building sites and sold them on to new users or residents who then would pay the annual dues directly to the Campbells.

Setting out

With the guidance of engineer James Cook, Harley began setting out the new streets in Blythswood and Garnethill. At the same time his own new Establishment next to (Upper) Nile Street expanded, housing his new businesses selling water, providing baths, developing

Entrance to the New Club, West George Street, painting by Robert Eadie.

a dairy, and building a bakery. His textile manufacturing continued and his Blythswood Pleasure Gardens grew grander. The family estimate that in today's money Harley invested over £20 million in setting out Blythswood Hill. There was a reasonable prospect of achieving rich reward as each steading (meaning a building site, which could be an entire city block) was completed and occupied. The writer Senex states that 'he tastily laid off and improved the whole grounds he had feued.'

The streets were bottomed with hard clinker transported from the furnaces of iron foundries, to be finished with whinstone. (The clinker ash was used to improve the fields.) The pavements were finished with flagstones. Mews lanes 16 feet wide were added once house building started on a block. Also known as Meuse lanes from the old French word meaning a place for hiding things, the lanes gave access to the occupant's back garden, stables and gig-house. Some developers near Renfield Street and on Garnethill opted instead to form a decorative garden square for residents. The largest such square would soon be developed on the summit of Blythswood by William Harley.

War and peace

Nobody thought that the French Wars, first begun in 1792, would keep continuing. Napoleon's desire for a European Empire to his aims greatly prolonged the wars and costs to Britain and others – for over twenty years until peace was confirmed by the success of the Battle of Waterloo in 1815. The return of so many soldiers and sailors to an exhausted country with its stagnating trade brought well over a decade of major recession and social unrest. Land values across Britain fell by 40 per cent. It was the spread of the railways in the 1830s which boosted the expansion of trade.

Many of the new Blythswood streets took names reflecting the naval and military victories in the French Wars, the new peace being vital to Glasgow's international trading. These include Nile Street, St Vincent Street, Hope Street (originally Copenhagen Street), Waterloo Street and Wellington Street. Other streets took the name or places of the Campbell/ Douglas families such as Renfield Street, Renfrew Street, Bothwell Street, West Campbell Street, Douglas Street and Blythswood Street (originally Mains Street).

Marocheti's fine equestrian statue of the Duke of Wellington graces the front of the Royal Exchange in Queen Street. One of its leading promoters in the 1820s was Alexander Downie, the first occupant of 10 Blythswood Square and business partner of Charles Macintosh inventor of the waterproof raincoat.

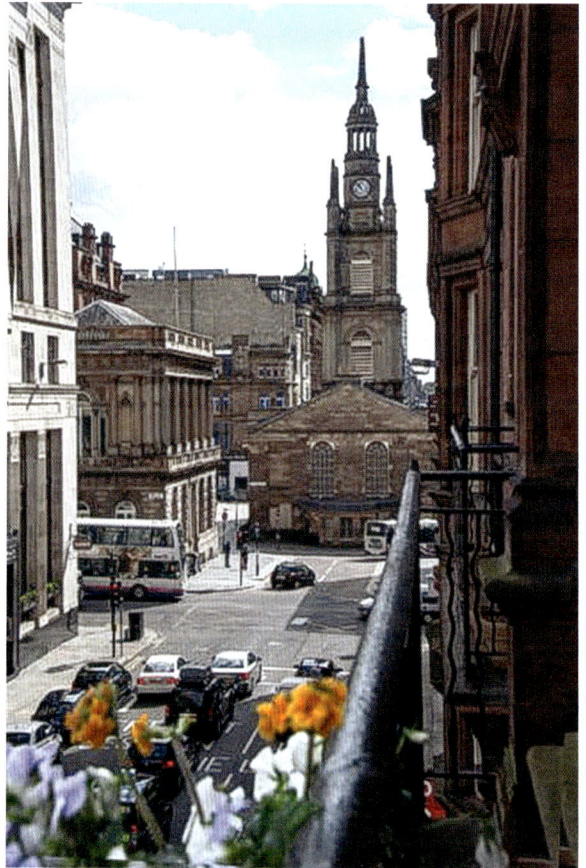

St George's Church viewed from West George Street, and West Nile Street which follows the line of Enoch Burn.

Duke of Wellington on his horse Copenhagen, in front of the Royal Exchange, sculpture by Carlo Marochetti.

Chapter 12

First New Houses

St Vincent Street, with Blythswood Place centre left extending down to Hope Street, viewing east to beyond George Square. The University's tower stands above High Street, engraving by Joseph Swan, 1828.

From 1810, after setting out his streets, William Harley started the building of houses. Fine villas appeared on the south-facing slope of Garnethill, with large gardens cascading to Sauchiehall road.

His first three terraces of three-storeyed townhouses, with front gardens, followed the line of Sauchiehall road on its south side. Each house had two public rooms, five bedrooms, bath and water closet, and in the sunken level was the kitchen, laundry and washing house etc; all 'enclosed with shrubbery in front and bleaching green behind.'

Robert Chapman's Guide to Glasgow in 1820 describes William Harley's active enterprises in Bath Street, noting: 'To the west of this establishment, the same gentleman has erected a range of buildings, combining a degree of elegance with the retirement of the country. Each house is occupied by one family, and the whole is laid off in a regular and uniform manner, divided into Wellington-Place, Windsor-Place, and Kensington-Place.'

The firm of Gavin Lindsay carried out the masonry work and the supplier of iron work and railings was the Edington family of Phoenix Iron Works, the first major foundry in Glasgow. By the 1820s there were 23 foundries in and around the city, all busy at work. Very soon there would be 1800 masons working on Blythswood Hill.

Corner of Blythswood Square and Douglas Street.

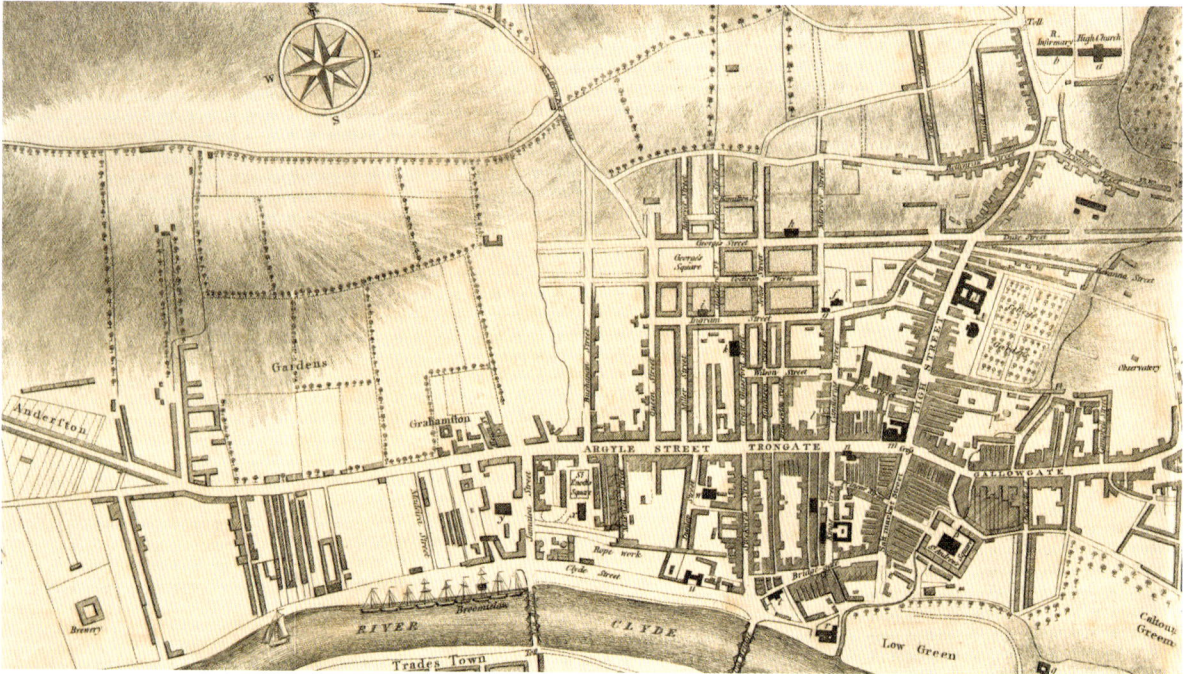

James Denholm map of 1797 illustrating the hills and expanse of empty lands west of Buchanan Street.

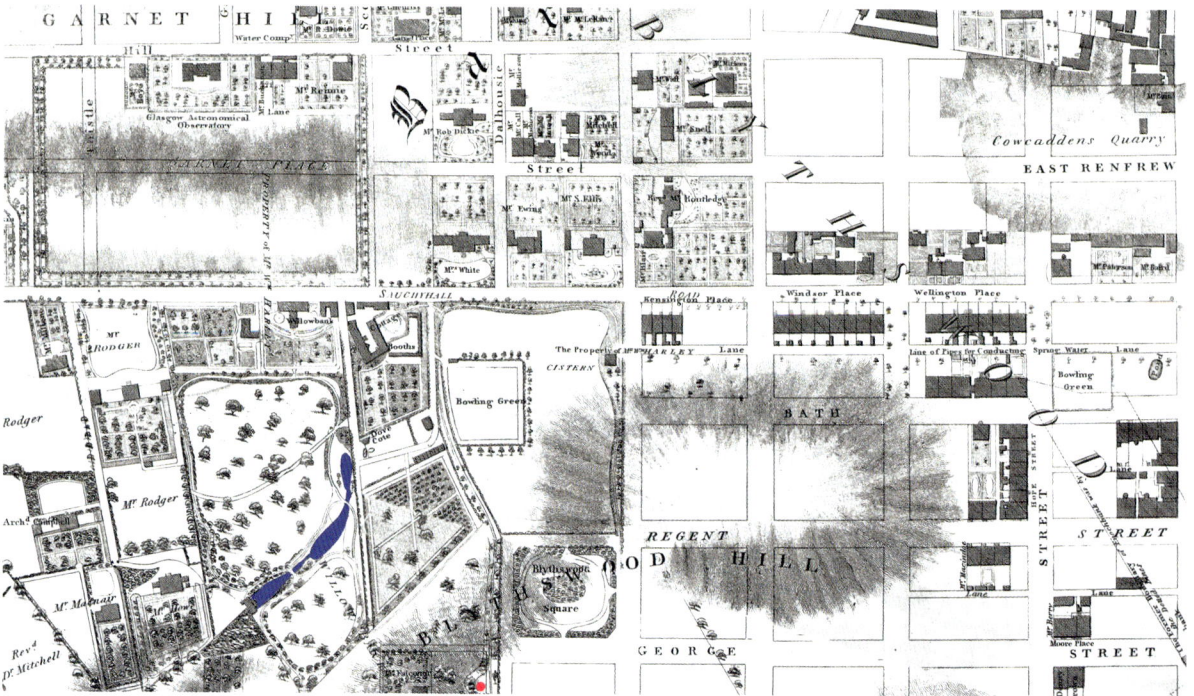

David Smith map of 1821 centred on Sauchyhall Road showing much of William Harley's land to the north, south and east.

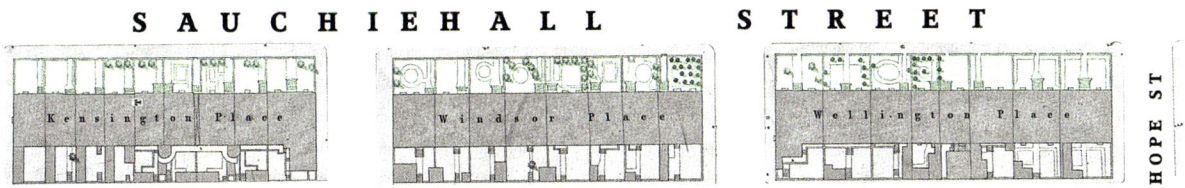

S A U C H I E H A L L   S T R E E T

Kensington Place   Windsor Place   Wellington Place   HOPE ST

William Harley's first housing mapped on Sauchiehall Street, the terraced townhouses of Wellington Place, Windsor Place and Kensington Place, stretching west from Hope Street to Blythswood Street.

Compared with James Denholm's 1797 map of Glasgow, showing the vast empty lands of the unnamed Blythswood Hill and Garnet Hill west of Buchanan Street, David Smith's map of 1821 shows the area now named Blythswood Hill and Garnet Hill. Streets have been lined out and some housing adorns the steadings closest to 'Sauchyhall' road, bordered on the east by Nile Street with the Enoch Burn flowing under it.

Along the Sauchyhall
Along the Sauchyhall can be seen William Harley's residence of Willow Bank and its outbuildings, with his sculpted Pleasure Gardens stretching south past the hill's summit and down towards Anderston. He has formed Blythswood Square, ready for its four stylish terraces.

Terraces being built over the first three decades of the new century often had their own name as the main address, such as Adelaide Place and Willowbank Place in Bath Street, Blythswood Place in St Vincent Street, and Moore Place in West George Street. Houses covered most of the area although newspapers carried Dean of Guild reports in the 1840s that 'some buildings were being disguised in to shops in Sauchiehall road and St Vincent Street.'

By the late 1870s the first named terraces, Wellington, Windsor and Kensington on the south side of Sauchiehall Street, from Hope Street to Blythswood Street, would give way to major palaces of art and commerce in that thoroughfare, namely the Royal Glasgow Institute of the Fine Arts and its new Gallery, the iconic departmental warehouses of Copland & Lye, Pettigrew & Stephens – which was the largest store in the city – Daly's and numerous adjacent boutiques and tearooms.

Lower down Blythswood
Lower down Blythswood on a steading sold by William Harley the first new terrace of townhouses there was named Blythswood Place, constructed in 1816. This enjoyed the sunny aspect of the north side of St Vincent Street, just west of Hope Street. The first occupant at No.1 Blythswood Place (today 140 St Vincent Street) was a prosperous hat-maker and West India merchant, Thomas Dunlop Douglas, previously living in Glassford Street. He had bought and built the entire street block, retiring in 1845 when he purchased Dunlop estate in Ayrshire, once the family's ancestral land.

Many more blocks would follow and from the *Glasgow Herald* an advertisement to let, furnished, reads: 'An elegant and commodious House in Blythswood Hill, consisting of Dining Room, Drawing Room, Ante-Drawing Room, Parlour, and Six Bed Rooms, Kitchen, Laundry, and Servants' Rooms, Bath, Store Room, and Wine Cellar, with Washing House and Green. Rent moderate.'

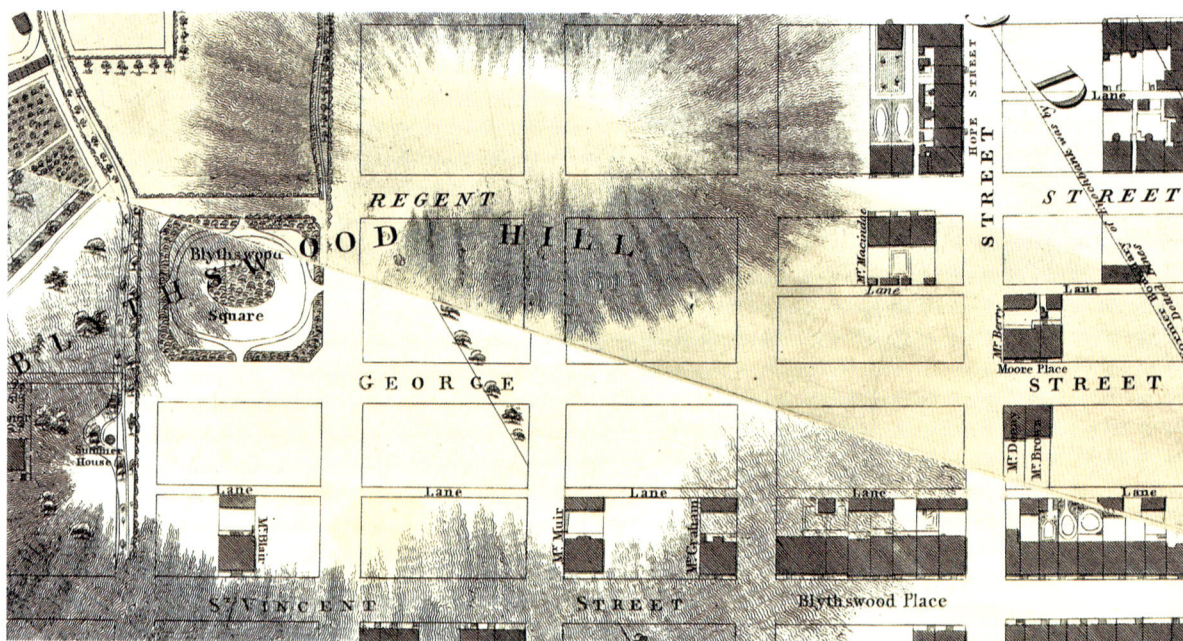

David Smith map of 1821 showing Blythswood Square, newly laid out, to St Vincent Street being built.

Immediately south of Harley's outlined Blythswood Square, the first house high up on Blythswood Hill enjoyed an open outlook over the Clyde from St Vincent Street. Built in 1819, this was the home of the Blair family. For a time their address in Glasgow directories was simply: 'Blair, merchant, house on the Hill, Blythswood.' It was given a number, 242 St Vincent Street, and continues today as the centre of the Royal College of Physicians and Surgeons of Glasgow.

The new privately owned Glasgow Bank, led by merchants James Dennistoun and Robert Blair, had bought from Harley the south facing block fronting St Vincent Street. (They also bought the north-facing block a couple of years later.) The first house here in its middle was built for the Blair family and stood on its own for many years. The full length was duly built upon with terraced townhouses except for the west side of 242. That

would be built later in Victorian style as the splendid Windsor Hotel, remaining as one of Glasgow's top hotels until the arrival of major railway hotels at Central station and St Enoch station.

On the summit

On the very summit of Blythswood, William Harley reduced the height of the hill by thirty feet to accommodate a level square of housing and gardens, tipping the spoil further south and west to the ravine towards the Elmbank Street of the future. The Campbells' surveyor records on his estate plans the new square gardens as 'Plot 118A Central Area of the Square now forming by Mr Harley.'

By 1830 one third of the property rental wealth of Glasgow was now in Blythswood Town, and not in the royal burgh boundaries, with a large loss of local tax-income to the council.

Amateur Concert, The Looking Glass, 1825.

Sauchiehall Street villas and their gardens on the north side, and newly built tenements on the south, viewing west to Park and Trinity College, about 1860.

Miss Kate Cranston's Willow Tearooms in Sauchiehall Street, sitting on the former Kensington Place.

Sauchiehall Street looking east around 1910. The quality tearooms and elegant stores on the right, all the way to Hope Street, replaced Harley's first three terraces of townhouses.

4. La Trenise.

Evening Fashions & New Quadrilles, The Looking Glass, 1825.

Chapter 13

The Blair Family and 242 St Vincent Street

242 St Vincent Street, now home of the Royal College of Physicians and Surgeons of Glasgow.

Beyond shipping and commerce, poetry and philosophy featured in the life of the Blairs, first occupants of 242 St Vincent Street.

Robert Blair, who bought it for the family, was of the firm of Stiven, Blair & Company, gingham, pullicate and muslin manufacturers, a business about the same size as William Harley's. His late brother David, a naval officer, East India merchant and partner in the business, had married Janet Muir, who was a sister-in-law of the Stiven family. She was of the Muirs of Huntershill (today's Bishopbriggs) and sister of the advocate Thomas Muir. As a presbyterian, Thomas supported the rights of man. He spoke passionately in favour of parliamentary democracy and ending monarchy. He was hailed as a friend by the newly formed United States of America.

Possibly the younger Blairs were the first to move to the 'New Town of Blythswood' from the setting of South Charlotte Street and its eleven mansions designed by Robert Adam in the 1780s, complete with its gated roadway next to Glasgow Green. Neighbours there included the family of David Dale and the family of Rev Dr John Lockhart. From 242 St Vincent Street Janet Muir Blair's daughter Louisa married a son of the Rev Lockhart, becoming part of Sir Walter Scott's circle. Louisa's brothers Thomas and James progressed as master mariners.

It was 1827 when the lyrical poet, educator and champion of Polish independence, Thomas Campbell (whose statue is in George Square) was again installed as Lord Rector of the University, in the High Street. The poet was guest of honour at a celebration dinner hosted by James Blair at no. 242. There, silver-plate was presented to Campbell by a group of fifty students and his health toasted. The poet finished his reply with an epigram: 'Said the South to the North, I surpass you, my friend,/With all the advantage your mountains can lend; Because not a nightingale sings in your sky,/Then the North to the South made immediate reply: Let your nightingales warble—I envy them not./While I list to the strains of my BURNS and my SCOTT !'

Louisa Blair and the Scott family

When in 1825 Louisa Blair married the young Rev Lawrence Lockhart, they set up home in the manse of Inchinnan Church, parish kirk of the Campbells of Blythswood House. She became an in-law of Sir Walter Scott whose daughter Sophia had married the minister's brother John Gibson Lockhart, future biographer of Scott. The novelist was a regular visitor to Glasgow, home of his mother's relatives and kinsman of the Blythswood Campbells. Walter Scott's journal records many visits including one in September 1827:

At Glasgow (Buck's Head) we met Mrs Maclean Clephane and her two daughters, and there was much joy. After the dinner the ladies sung, particularly Anna Jane, who has more taste and talent of every kind than half the people going with great reputations on their back. A very pleasant day was paid for by a restless night. [The following day]...... Went down by steam to Colonel Campbell's, Blythswood House, where I was received most courteously by him and his sisters. We are kinsfolk and very old acquaintance. His seat here is a fine one; the house is both grand and comfortable.

We walked to Lawrence Lockhart's of Inchinnan, within a mile of Blythswood House. It is extremely nice and comfortable, far beyond the style of a Scotch clergyman; but Lawrence is wealthy. I found John Lockhart and Sophia there, returned from Largs. We all dined at Colonel Campbell's on turtle, and all manner of good things. The sleep at night made amends for the Buck's Head.

The youngest of Louisa's children, all born in Inchinnan, was General Sir William Lockhart.

South Charlotte Street at Glasgow Green, painting by David Small, 1845.

Thomas Campbell, portrait by Sir Thomas Lawrence.

Sir Walter Scott, portrait after Sir Thomas Lawrence.

Starting as a cadet in the East India Company he rose through the ranks to become Commander-in-Chief of Her Majesty's forces in India.

Captain Blair

Thomas Blair, always known as Captain Blair, was a commander of ships of the Honourable East India Company. His ships were owned by Fairlie & Co, one of many merchant firms of Scots in Calcutta, and the largest shipowner. The cargoes included rice, indigo, cotton, tea and opium. After William Fairlie retired, the business became known as Jardine, Matheson. One ship of particular size and note from 1821 onwards was the HEIC *William Fairlie*. The Fairlie family would retire to their native Ayrshire, creating Coodham mansion and its estate. Their son James Fairlie noted the complete lack of golf courses in the area – he had been used to Calcutta Golf Club – and instructed the making of Prestwick Golf course. He and the Earl of Eglinton went on to found the Open Golf championship.

Captain Blair was generous to a fault. The Irish-born actor and esteemed playwright Sheridan Knowles settled in Glasgow. A son, Dr James Knowles. recalls:

> Amongst my father's many Glasgow friends was Captain Thomas Blair, of the Hon. East India Company's navy. One night after they had supped together prior to Captain Blair's starting the next day on a voyage to Calcutta, as they were bidding each other good-bye, Blair placed in my father's hands a roll of bank-notes, with these words: 'If we never meet again, Knowles, regard this as a legacy.' It was £500. Some time before

HEIC Walter Fairlie, commanded by Captain Thomas Blair, leaving the harbour of George Town, Penang, painting by William John Huggins, 1826.

this, seeing my father struggling with a large family, and being himself a bachelor and very wealthy, he offered to adopt one of his sons, and provide for him. But you might as well ask my father to give you his heart out of his breast as to part, even to such a friend and on such terms, with one of his children. So that offer went off. 'Well, then,' said Blair, 'bring up your eldest son to the medical profession, and as soon as he is qualified, I will get him an appointment in my own ship.'

This was done, and he joined the *William Fairlie*.

'Our heritage the sea'
The circle of friends included a young writer, Allan Cunningham, son of a tenant farmer next to Robert Burns' farm in Dumfries. He enthused over Burns' work and was mentored by Sir Walter Scott, becoming a novelist, poet and biographer. Two of his maritime poems are *To Captain Blair, On his Sailing to China* and in the same metre and wording *A Wet Sheet and a Flowing Sea*. This was later set to music and has become the best known sea-song in the English speaking world.

In 1830 in Calcutta, Captain Blair married Matilda, daughter of Charles Mackenzie, a senior merchant of the Hon. East India Company. A few years later the Captain decided he would retire and 'come ashore' in Glasgow

General Sir William Lockhart, Commander-in-Chief of the Indian Army, and youngest son of Louisa Blair; The Illustrated London News, 1897.

Port of Calcutta in the 1830s, painting by Sir Charles D'Oyly.

after his next long and hazardous voyage to the Orient. Before embarking in late 1833 he rode on horseback from St Vincent Street to see his sister Louisa in Inchinnan. Tragically, just before reaching Inchinnan, he fell off his horse and died of a fractured skull. A few months later his wife gave birth to their second child, Thomasina Matilda Blair.

Captain James Blair and the times of Thomas Muir

James Blair was also a sea captain and merchant, wisely marrying into an Admiral's family. For much of his time he was based in the south-west of England.

Up to the 1790s the Blairs' uncle, advocate Thomas Muir, was prominent in promoting political democracy and supported the French Revolution. Unfortunately France declared war on countries all around it. He and others went on trial in 1793 at the High Court in Edinburgh accused of sedition, facing a judge who had already made up his mind and a jury rigged by the judge. All were found guilty and sentenced to transportation. Muir was despatched to the penal colony of Botany Bay in Australia for 14 years. After two years there he managed to find a ship journeying to Spanish California. He made his way across the continent and avoided capture when sailing to Spain, finally settling in France.

James Blair retired back to Glasgow, now staying in Bath Street as 242 St Vincent Street had been given up. A few years after the

Reform Act of 1832 was passed he supported the plans, started by the chemical manufacturer Charles Tennant and others, to commemorate the political martyrs of which Thomas Muir was the most famous. Eventually the fine, tall obelisk to the Political Martyrs was paid for and inscribed, constructed in 1845 in Edinburgh's Old Calton burial-ground. A second memorial to the Political Martyrs is in Nunhead Cemetery, London.

Cartoon of a nautch party hosted by Raja Nob Kishen in Calcutta around 1820, by Sir Charles D'Oyly.

Royal College of Physicians and Surgeons of Glasgow

The Royal College, founded in 1599, represents its world-wide members in medicine, surgery, dentistry and allied fields. It sets professional standards and promotes multi-disciplinary education. In the 1860s the Faculty, as it was known, moved from St Enoch Square to number 242 St Vincent Street. Over time it has acquired all the adjoining townhouses in the block.

As a postgraduate institution it presents, here and overseas, courses, lectures conferences and licentiate examinations. The College library and medical collections are of national importance. Each year a series of exhibitions is usually open to members of the public.

In the 1890s the College buildings were adapted and enhanced by architect Sir John James Burnet including the splendid College Hall added to the rear of the terrace. At the front, the Princess Alexandra salon on the first floor above the entrance to 242 would be largely recognisable by the Blair family if they returned today.

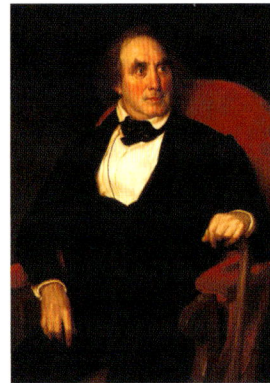

Sheridan Knowles, portrait by Wilhelm Trautschold.

Thomas Muir of Huntershill, profile by John Kay.

The Princess Alexandra salon of the Royal College of Physicians and Surgeons of Glasgow.

The College Hall of the Royal College of Physicians and Surgeons of Glasgow, designed by Sir John James Burnet.

Chapter 14

Money Matters and the Smith Family

The north terrace of Blythswood Square, photograph by Thomas Annan, 1857.

All of William Harley's new businesses and land development were funded by himself. By 1811 he still had surplus money in his Bank of Scotland account. However the growing recession and continuing wars meant people had less money to spend, especially for moving to a new house. By 1815 he was running out of cash.

In 1816 Harley signed a voluntary trust deed with his suppliers. By agreement he paid eight shillings and nine pence in the pound to settle his debts and continue business. The largest amount owed was to the engineer James Cook. William Harley was now joined by voluntary trustees to help complete the land development in a profitable way.

Around this time he took a loan from the Ship Bank and smaller loan from the Royal Bank of Scotland. Meanwhile the Campbells of Blythswood with ample money and time got into the habit of frequently taking developers to the most expensive court in the land, the Court of Session, for their own advantage. After 1816 Harley fell into arrears in paying feu-duties to the Campbells. In 1818 he owed about a year and a half's worth and had sought time to pay.

In court the Campbells agreed that 'by honest mistake' the sale of the thirty five acres to William Harley included Sauchyhall road but it was a public road and not theirs to sell. The amount refunded to Harley paid for more than a third of the outstanding feu-duties!

In Edinburgh the Court of Directors of the Royal Bank of Scotland formed a committee specially to monitor Harley's progress in turning things around. They were kindly disposed to him and gave him time. However in October 1821 the bank concluded that matters would likely go 'from bad to worse' and that sequestration of his business and personal assets should go ahead, commencing in 1822. John Smith, architect and mason, was appointed to take charge. Harley's various businesses were duly sold off, some developments continued and numerous plots in Blythswood and Garnethill were sold at very low prices.

The Campbells, as historical land superior, smelt blood and, with visions of more pots of gold ahead, tried to grab land back. They defended themselves at the Court of Session claiming that as Harley and trustees had not received the approval of the Campbell surveyor, William Kyle, to each

The north terrace of Blythswood Square today.

Sauchiehall Street looking east to Tréron's and the McLellan Galleries.

property sale then all property transactions should be declared null and void and all the land should revert back to the Campbells. The judge said no, clarifying what was unclear across Scotland now that cities were greatly expanding and new areas being developed. Harley was required to **notify** William Kyle of each sale but there was no need to seek prior approval.

In the 1920s, David Murray, a founder of the law firm McLay, Murray & Spens, donated to Glasgow University Library his collection of 20,000 books and pamphlets charting the growth and social life of Glasgow. In the frontispiece of one book of the time he writes in splendid copper-plate about 'William Harley – the Great Improver':

Glasgow owed much to William Harley, baths, water and dairies; and the actions (Harley v Campbell) which practically settled that a feuar is not bound to employ the superior's agent to prepare conveyances of the land feued.

The Smith family

John Smith was well regarded in all spheres of construction. His son James Smith became a prominent architect, and son-in-law of the eminent David Hamilton who was the father figure of architects in Glasgow and the West of Scotland – his largest work being Hamilton Palace for the Duke of Hamilton. James and his wife moved to no.6/7 Blythswood Square, the north terrace. Madeleine Smith, their dark-haired twenty-one-year old daughter, would gain national headlines day after day when she was tried at the High Court in 1857 for the alleged homicide of her lover.

Madeleine Smith.

Madeleine Smith on trial in court.

In Glasgow, John Smith had earlier been appointed by the Royal Bank of Scotland to finalise the building of Royal Exchange Square after its main architect David Hamilton ran out of money. Now appointed in 1822 by the Royal Bank as the statutory trustee of the bankrupted Harley he oversaw the completion of unfinished houses and granted new contracts to finish other immediate terraces. He settled disputes and authorised the auction of surplus steadings and plots. Overall his work on Blythswood continued into the 1840s.

Architect James Smith designed houses, country mansions, public buildings and some of Royal Exchange Square. In 1840 he designed Glasgow Collegiate School in Garnethill which appears to be the first purpose-built school in Harley's area. On the southside of Sauchiehall Street in the late 1840s he designed the tenements which stand where William Harley's Willow Bank house and outbuildings once were. In 1856 he designed the McLellan Art Galleries in Sauchiehall Street (greatly extended in the 1900s).

In July 1857, now a prisoner and not at home in Blythswood Square nor the family's seaside mansion in Rhu overlooking the Gareloch,

Madeleine Smith, eldest of the Smith daughters, stood trial accused of killing her lover Pierre Emile L'Angelier by arsenic poisoning. He was a packing clerk in a warehouse at no.10 Bothwell Street, and regarded by some as a social 'gold-digger.'

In a crowded courtroom the trial lasted nine days. As she sat in the dock, newspapers remarked that she had 'the air of a belle entering a ballroom or a box at the opera'. The Smith family engaged the most experienced and expensive defence team. Almost every detail of the clandestine romance and her passionate love letters over two years were reported in newspapers daily. The jury gave their verdict of 'not proven.' The public cheered and newspapers thought the verdict was right but mystery remained. Madeleine went on to marry twice, having family with her first husband who became the prosperous business manager of artist William Morris. She settled in New York, living to a ripe old age. Her descendants still live in the USA. Many books, films and plays have been written about Miss Smith.

Chapter 15

Blythswood Square

Top: Blythswood Square on the north side, in line with West Regent Street.
Bottom: The east side of Blythswood Square, remodelled for the Royal Scottish Automobile Club.

Blythswood Square is William Harley's urban jewel in the New Town, conceived and named by him. It was built in the 1820s after considerable height was taken off Blythswood Hill's summit to make space.

The Dunblane-born architect James Gillespie Graham, now based in Edinburgh, opened a Glasgow office at the top of Buchanan Street. He was well established in designing castles, stately homes, churches across Scotland and city terraces in Edinburgh. He was chosen by the Campbells to design their new stately abode, Blythswood House, at Renfrew. He also designed Drimsynie House, 'standing in a Lawn of nineteen acres', at the head of Loch Goil in the 5,300 acre estate the Campbells had bought some twenty years earlier. This was Archibald Campbell's coastal retreat, where he was already an elder in Lochgoilhead Kirk. The Campbells continued their townhouse in Miller Street.

The architect also penned for the Campbells a street layout of Blythswood Holm, the flatter lands just south of St Vincent Street, to be marketed as 'The Town of Blythswood extended agreeably'. For William Harley the architect sized and outlined Blythswood Square and an indication of the houses to be built.

Harley must have been impressed. He contacted his brother-in-law William

Drimsynie House, Lochgoilhead.

Blythswood Square from the south side, looking east down West George Street.

Blythswood House, Renfrew.

Laird in Birkenhead who then instructed Gillespie Graham to provide a layout and designs for the building of the new town of Birkenhead. The central part named Hamilton Square, is twice the size of Harley's Blythswood Square. The first of its terraces, designed by the architect, was built in 1826. The Town Hall was added in the 1880s.

Each of the houses in the terraces of Blythswood Square would be of four storeys with a choice of 'a Two Stalled Stable and Coachhouse behind'. A three-stalled stable was also possible. A family's coachman had high status among servants and was paid £30 a year.

It is thought that the house elevations were set out by architect John Brash, who also designed the fine corner townhouse today known as 196 West George Street. Most houses would have eleven main rooms. Some houses at street corners were flatted, with fewer main rooms, to suit purchasers. The principal building contractor employed over the next few years was the firm of James McCulloch jnr.

Gas pipes would be installed mainly for lighting, but not in bedrooms for reasons of safety. For heating and cooking, coal was 6d a waggon. There would be a choice of piped water; either spring water from Willow-Bank supplied to the ground level or from the new rival Water Companies supplied to each level thanks to the new Cranstonhill reservoir tank built on the top of Garnethill.

As was the custom, the drawing-room in each house was upstairs on the first floor at the front, and servants' rooms in the basement. The terrace built on the west side had the drawing-rooms at the back of the houses with superb views of the countryside and the setting sun.

Promotion of his latest development got underway including advertisements in newspapers such as the *Glasgow Herald*. Harley never missed a trick.

COMING SOON and views from the Summer House

NOTICE

THE SQUARE at BLYTHSWOOD HILL is now formed, and the road cut to communicate with St Vincent Street.

Those who wish to ascertain the view from the Houses to be built round the Square, will have access to the Summer House every lawful day from 3pm to 4pm, and Saturday from 2 to dusk.

From recent arrangements the public will now get a full supply of WILLOW BANK BREAD and BISCUITS. The Company use nothing but the best of Flour, and have excellent tradesmen, whose conduct, as well as all employed about Willow Bank, both in and without doors, has been exemplary, as they continued at their work during the late disturbance.

THE BATHS and BALCONY continue open as usual.

The Bowling Greens are now open. Subscribers will have access to both Greens unless the old one should be broken up – The subscription to be paid in advance.

A commodious LODGING to LET or SELL.

On Sale,

GRAVEL for WALKS

Willow Bank, 7th April 1820.

The disturbance noted was part of the widespread strikes of hand loom weavers and others in 1820. Radical calls for franchise reform brought military reaction.

ELEVATIONS now on display in the Tontine

NEW SQUARE, &c

THE ELEVATIONS for BUILDING the SQUARE on BLYTHSWOOD HILL may now be seen in the Tontine Coffee Room. The interior of the Square is finished with Gravel Walks, Shrubs &c. As the GROUND falls on all sides, the delightful views can never be interrupted.

For particulars, apply to Messrs. Graham, Cuthill, and Monteath, 51, Miller Street; or to Mr Harley.

FAMILIES returning to town, and the community at large, may have a liberal supply of WILLOW-BANK BREAD and MILK, the quality of which has been found very superior; and the cleanliness of the Establishments, and manner of conducting them, give high satisfaction to the numerous strangers who daily visit them.

WILLOW-BANK, 28th August, 1820.

The Tontine, next to the Tolbooth at Glasgow Cross, was the main business Exchange for the city before the building of the Royal Exchange at Queen Street.

ELEGANCE with a delightful prospect

ELEGANT SQUARE, &c
ON SALE

THAT SQUARE on BLYTHSWOOD HILL, conformable to the elevations now exhibiting in the Tontine Coffee Room.

The delightful prospect, fine air, and good access, render this site peculiarly desirable as a Town and Country residence. The houses can be supplied with water from either of the Companies, or with the spring water of Willow Bank. As there is no Feu upon the ground, it is an eligible property for those who have money to invest.

Apply to Messrs. Graham, Cuthill, and Monteath, 51 Miller Street, or to W. Harley.

....

W.HARLEY feels grateful for the increasing patronage given to the BATHS, DAIRY and BAKING ESTABLISHMENTS. Both the Milk and the Bread have been repeatedly examined and found of superior quality.

WILLOW-BANK, 6th October, 1820.

VALUABLE and HANDSOME

Valuable Property TO BE SOLD: the SQUARE on BLYTHSWOOD HILL, conformable to a ground plan by Wm. Kyle, and handsome elevations by eminent Architects.

As this site is unrivalled, both disposer and purchaser will be bound to observe Uniformity in building. When a builder or individual should purchase a compartment they will have liberty to make an elevation to please themselves, under certain limitations.

For particulars apply to Messrs. Graham, Cuthill, Monteath; Mr Henry Paul, accountant; or to Mr W. Harley.

The NEW BOWLING GREEN is now open. The Subscription Book lies at the Bath Office.

Admission to view the COWS and INDIAN CATTLE as formerly.

BREAD and BISCUITS to be had from the Shops, or sent to order.

WILLOW-BANK, 30th March, 1821.

Hamilton Square, Birkenhead.

Tontine Hotel, Trongate.

The west side of Blythswood Square.

Unfortunately Harley was bankrupted in 1822. His voluntary trustees continued with developments for a few years. Advertising in 1826 describes one of the elegant lodgings on the south side of the square 'lately possessed by Mr William Ewing and containing Dining Room, Drawing Room, Parlour, Eight Bed Rooms, Kitchen, Laundry, Servants' Rooms, Butler's Pantry, Larder, Wine and Beer Cellars, with other conveniences' on sale at £2,400. The last terrace to be completed was the north side in 1829.

What happened to Harley's trustees?

The voluntary trustees assisting William Harley from 1816 to promote the building and selling of houses and to make some profit included lawyers, accountants, merchants and the civil engineer James Cook. Of these, several met financial failure the same as Harley. They included merchant Hamilton William Garden;

Archibald Cuthill who was a lawyer and speculative builder; and the patient James Cook.

Hamilton William Garden was a son of a Tobacco Lord family who tip-toed in and out of bankruptcy. He longed to become the main developer, announcing the square would be now known as Garden Square, modest man that he was. He would rename the top of Douglas Street as Alston Place after his wife, whose family owned the lands where Central Station would be built. Jane Street, just off Blythswood Square, was named after their daughter.

Garden bought from the trustees most of the considerable lands remaining in the Harley trust in 1822 which Garden said he would build on immediately. (He also bought land at the western edges of Harley's Blythswood.) This was agreed as a substantial free loan from the trustees to be paid back by Garden as and when houses were completed in Blythswood Square and nearby streets. A condition was that two thirds of the houses in the Square were to be completed by 1823. But they were not and he was bankrupted in 1826, whereupon he and his wife sped off to America.

Houses which he did sell went for around 10% less than the amount needed to cover their cost. The square resumed its proper name as Blythswood Square. John Smith, for the Royal Bank and others, had already taken over the main task of winding up Harley's affairs.

Archibald Cuthill had built houses in the 1790s in and off Glassford Street where he lived, followed by new housing in Hutchesontown, and from 1819 on Blythswood Hill. As a new

View from North-west corner of Blythswood Square, engraving by Allan & Ferguson in 1843, with Elmbank Crescent to date in left foreground and Woodlands Hill and Claremont centre right.

trustee Cuthill continued to build on Harley land, aided by loans from James Cook and banks. To avoid facing his debts Cuthill fled to France in 1826. It was then discovered that Cuthill had also secretly worked his way through his wife's large fortune from her first husband, an East India merchant who owned Kelvinside estate.

James Cook was a man of integrity, like Harley. He too built on the Hill in his own name – after Harley – and had overseen its civil engineering but the national recession, and some dubious fellow-trustees, meant there was little prospect of seeing his invested money returning. His pockets had been deep thanks to his engineering business in Tradeston but the recession started to affect it too.

On his passing in 1833 the business went to his general manager David Cook (no relation) at a valuation of nil.

Slopes, songs and schooling

On Blythswood Hill some of the intersecting streets running south/north have steep slopes near Bothwell Street. So much so that carters complained it was difficult to take loads up them, especially in wintry weather, and that horses' legs were at risk.

Schooling was largely in the houses of teachers or in new academies operating within some of the buildings. Many had the good fortune of a governess in the family's own townhouse. There were soon school halls attached to the many new churches. Purpose built schooling would start firstly in Garnethill in 1840 and then Elmbank Street in 1847.

Soirees and music held sway in the city. Newspapers reflected on the era in the 1830s when the new opera *Masaniello* by Daniel Auber became a regular visitor to Glasgow. It first opened in the Theatre Royal, then situated in York Street in a building owned by ship owner John Laird, William Harley's brother-in-law. 'In this building *Masaniello* was first performed in Glasgow with the famous John Braham in the title-part. The opera was repeated again and again in the town with undiminished success. The music was immensely popular, as well it may be. Young ladies in the West-end strummed it on their pianos [the West-end terminated at Blythswood-square], street boys whistled the "Market Chorus" and barrel organs ground out the "barcarolle" and the "guaracha".'

With the impetus given by Harley, others started planning new developments even further west, most notably in the late 1830s when Claremont and Woodlands Hill got underway.

The acres of Blythswood land to be built on took many years for completion. The open space and streets along Blythswood Holm and up to Great Western Road were used for recreation at this time by a growing population that included wealthy adults with time for sports, and children playing on the sites laid out for building. Campbell's factor tried his best to keep order. Eventually in 1847 the Blythswood Estate Office in St George's Place had to place a public notice in newspapers:

HORSES & RIDERS

NOTICE.

It has been the practice for some time past of exercising Horses and riding furiously upon the streets, footpaths, &c and through the unfeued grounds in Blythswood Holm: also riding and trespassing on the grass lands and unfeued grounds lying in the vicinity of Buccleuch Street, Woodland Road, Great Western Road, and other grounds upon the estate of Blythswood. It is requested that those practices will not be persevered in any longer.

Flights through time

Following Queen Victoria's first visit to Glasgow, in 1849, it was suggested (without success) that a Victoria Tower be built on Blythswood Hill in the centre of Blythswood Square in the same way as London, Dublin and Edinburgh had celebration towers. This would be about 30 feet high 'having a spiral stair inside, with a railed in gallery at the top, whence a view could be obtained, in one glance, of the magnitude of the city. Visitors would really see Glasgow, and not only Glasgow, but the vast expanse of the rich and picturesque valley of the Clyde from Tinto to the peaks of Arran. A grand Victoria column in Blythswood-square would attract visitors to the west and best end, affording a magnificent bird's-eye view of the entire city, with its river, bridges, and wide-stretching suburbs; and this from a point which promises to become pretty nearly the centre of our great and growing city'.

Britain's first telephone exchange started in 1879 in Douglas Street, initially for members of the medical profession. Competing companies merged in the coming decades with the first three letters of each district exchange being the dialling code such as CENtral, CITy, BELl, SOUth etc and DOUglas reflecting the Blythswood area.

By the end of the century, there were some 37 consuls in Glasgow representing foreign countries – from Argentina to the German Empire, Greece to Japan, and Siam to the USA. Of these, 30 were based on Blythswood Hill.

In the early 1900s the newly formed Scottish Automobile Club, suggested in Glasgow and convened in Edinburgh, started buying up houses on the east side of the Square. The first clubhouse occupied no. 11, opening in 1910. Finally in the 1920s the architect James Miller combined and remodelled the entire block, making it the splendid Royal Scottish Automobile Club, the largest and most elegant club in Scotland. Today it is the Blythswood Square Hotel.

Two years into WWII the nation and cities started thinking ahead about post war reconstruction. In Glasgow the City Engineer, Robert Bruce, headed a committee to devise a master plan, selecting the style of Le Corbusier, and published it in 1945. This proposed the wholesale demolition of the city centre and inner suburbs, including George Square, the City Chambers and even Kelvingrove Art Galleries & Museum. The Bruce Report planned for a new civic centre at Blythswood Square, complete with new city chambers. This thinking was trailed in 1943 when Dr Tom Honeyman, director of Kelvingrove, advocated that a municipal theatre and concert hall should be built on the south side of Blythswood Square, facing over the Clyde.

In 1948 the authorities proposed creating a helicopter pad in Blythswood Square as the base for new helicopter flights linking with international air services at Prestwick Airport. By the early 1960s car travel and the need for parking was a challenge. The motoring organisations suggested an underground car park below the Gardens, as is the case in some cities. The plans for it were first prepared in 1938, with thoughts of being useful for Civil Defence purposes.

Thanks to public pressure and the new Civic Amenities Act, Blythswood Square became one of the first two Conservation Areas of Glasgow in 1970 – to help safeguard areas of special architectural and historical interest. The other one was the Park Circus area. Blythswood, Garnethill and Park are now part of the wider Central Conservation Area.

A Good New Year, The Looking Glass, 1826.

Chapter 16

The Royal Scottish Automobile Club

Starting point of the Monte Carlo Rally, 1930s onwards, in front of the clubhouse.

The very new Scottish Automobile Club saw the light of day at a meeting in Edinburgh at the end of 1899, following an idea that year of its founding secretary Robert J Smith CA of 59 St Vincent Street, Glasgow. Newspapers reported the chairman's words: 'There was a great future for automobilism or mechanically-propelled carriages for purposes of pleasure, business and probably war. These were still in their infancy.'

The club set out 'to promote, encourage and develop automobilism in Scotland.'

Soon its members were more than half of the 'autocar' owners in Scotland, some in the eastern section based around Edinburgh and some in the western section based around Glasgow. Early runs, and subsequent rallies, took place across the country.

The new club actively promoted the interests of motorists and the new automobile industries. Numerous rallies, hill-climbing tests and competitions came to life over the coming decades, some in association with other clubs at home and overseas. Membership would rise to around 8,000 in the 1980s, enjoying also a swimming pool and fitness suite added to the club in Blythswood Square.

Attended by 11 million visitors over five months, it was the 1901 Glasgow International Exhibition in Kelvingrove, designed by James Miller, which helped display new manufacturing and models of cars and lorries, improving the acceptance of motoring and its benefits. There was a special week in September when the club presented the public with new delights: 'when autocars and distinguished automobilists from all parts of the world will meet for six days, on five of which runs, out from and back to the Exhibition, of average length of 100 miles each, will take place, the cars being shown in the evening, and all day on Saturday. Races will be held in the special track in the grounds, and about 100 of the latest types of autocars of all makes will compete for medals given by the Exhibition.'

Gang Warily, the crest and motto of the Royal Scottish Automobile Club above the entrance in Blythswood Square.

Car badge for members of the Royal Scottish Automobile Club.

Realising that the greater number of members were based in the west and that most engineering and automotive companies were likewise in the Glasgow area it was decided to centre its club premises here. Guided by the engineer and industrialist Lord Weir, a townhouse on the east side of Blythswood Square was bought in 1908. This was number 11, previously the home of artist Joseph Henderson, and club facilities opened for members and their families. As and when other houses in the terrace became available they too were bought by the club, and sometimes gifted. The last acquired, no.13 at the corner of West George Street, had in the mid-19th century been the home of carpet

Motor car parade on arrival back to the Sports stadium of the International Exhibition, 1901.

The first clubhouse of the Royal Scottish Automobile Club, at 11 Blythswood Square.

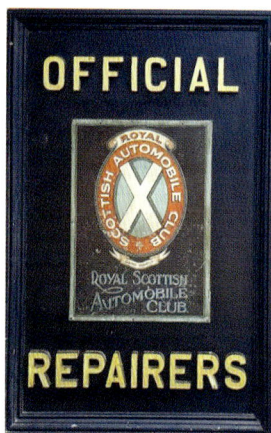

Hotels and garages were recommended by the Club; a style of the Official Repairers sign.

manufacturer A.F. Stoddard who had arrived in Glasgow from the USA.

When the Great War started in August 1914 the club set up and ran the transport committee of the Scottish Red Cross. Through 1914-1918, from gifts and public events, 450 ambulances were built or purchased, most forming ambulance convoys in France. In 1917 King George V bestowed to the club the prefix of 'Royal' in recognition of its significant contribution to the war effort.

Again in WWII the transport committee was reconvened and under the club's leadership 700 ambulances were provided for the Scottish Red

WWII Red Cross ambulances and lady drivers in Kelvin Way. (The author's mother-in-law was one such lady.)

Cross between 1939 and 1945. And the score of women driver volunteers of the First World War became an army of 500 for the Second. All in military uniform, they were club secretary A.K Stevenson's Young Ladies Corps (Red Cross Lady Drivers).

Under the presidency of Lord Weir, the club appointed architect James Miller to weave his magic through all six townhouses, numbers 8 to 13 in the 1920s. James Miller was one of the eminent Glasgow architects of national standing. He designed to suit his clients and the function of the buildings. He was superbly talented.

RSAC clubhouse, Blythswood Square, in the 1950s.

The entire building on the square's east side was combined and remodelled like a great Atlantic liner. So it should be, given that the Clyde was the world centre of shipbuilding. Just before WWI he had designed the palatial staterooms and passenger areas of Cunard's new liner *RMS Lusitania*, the fastest and most stylish ship afloat. Around the same time he designed the Anchor Line's headquarters in St Vincent Place

Entrance hall of the RSAC clubhouse, 1950s.

in similar quality and styling – today housing restaurants and accommodation.

The luxury clubhouse, opening during 1926, included a fully sprung ballroom which in winter would be used by members for afternoon tea dances and dinner dances. There was also garaging for 40 cars.

In WWII the square was taken over by the city council, its railings removed and a storage tank built in the middle to have water at hand for fighting incendiary bombs. After 1945 the club, and other proprietors, generously restored the gardens in the centre of the square, continuing their opening during daytime for public enjoyment.

James Miller's interior continues today, as the Blythswood Square Hotel. The spacious black and white marble floored entrance hall, with its classical columns, leads to the dining saloon and to the wide stairways to the floors above. Adorned by ranges of classical columns, the first floor has open lounges the full length of the building, from which are suites of rooms.

Starting point of the Monte Carlo Rally, 1930s onwards, in front of the clubhouse.

St Vincent Street.

Chapter 17

James Scott and Jane Galbraith

Top: Kelvingrove Park, about 1900. *Bottom*: Dalmonach Works, Bonhill, Vale of Leven.

James Scott.

James Scott, the prime developer of Bothwell Street and beyond, was born in Glasgow in 1810. He had the Midas touch in business and civic life.

From Falkirk, his father Thomas Scott had become a partner in the pioneering Rothesay Cotton Mills encouraged by the Marquis of Bute. When James reached sixteen he was a cotton broker. His mother's uncle introduced him to James Black & Co, calico printers, Glasgow, and by the age of twenty he was made a partner.

James Black & Co, with their offices and warehouse in Royal Exchange Square and print works in Dalmonach, Vale of Leven, were very profitable and used the most advanced science. It was first in Scotland able to print two colours at the one time. In the 1850s Black's was the first company in Britain to adopt the new colour dye of Tyrian Purple for calico printing, being fast colours of mauve and magenta. Later the company had machines printing sixteen different colours at one time, ahead of all else.

James Scott was one of the founders in 1833 of the Glasgow Church Building Society, which in its first five years or so erected twenty new churches in the expanding city. In the 1850s he was a donor to Glasgow Cathedral of one of the major new stained glass windows being commissioned from Munich.

For ten years to 1845 Scott was active in promoting railways to connect towns, manufacturers and districts, and ensuring freight could move easily to and from the quays on Clydeside. As part of this scheme he began buying considerable amounts of land suitable for development. This included Bothwell Street and Stobcross further west. Across on the southside of the river he bought the vast lands of Shieldhall next to Govan.

Family life and more public life

Retiring from daily business in 1847, he continued to own James Black & Company and be a major property developer. Marriage was next! In 1848 he married eighteen-year-old **Jane Galbraith**. She was born in Garnethill, a daughter of future Lord Provost Andrew Galbraith who was head of A. & A. Galbraith, cotton spinners and cloth manufacturers with their mills in Garngad and Oakbank. There, 350,000 yards of cloth were produced each week. They also had a mercantile house in Havana and Honduras. Family life started in Woodside Crescent, off Sauchiehall Street. The Scotts would have five sons and five daughters.

Seeking also a seaside residence, James Scott bought in the same year the estate and mansion of Kelly, sitting high above Wemyss Bay and looking over the Firth of Clyde. The estate had over 900 acres, with Kelly House having five public rooms, library, billiards room, eleven bedrooms, four dressing rooms and 'ample accommodation for Servants, with Coach House, Stables for Twelve Horses and etc.'

He became the leading promoter of the Wemyss Bay railway, its first pier and steamboat services. The railway's inaugural service in 1865 was advertised as being superior to the line which

Mrs James Scott of Kelly (Jane Galbraith), portrait by John Graham Gilbert, overlooking the Clyde and Arran.

Queen Margaret College, formerly North Park House.

served Greenock, as all the carriages contained seats! In 1866 he sold Kelly to Dr James 'Paraffin' Young, founder of the oil industry.

James Scott was too active in temperament to remain retired and returned to business. In 1852 James and his young brother William bought the extensive and valuable spinning and weaving mills in Bridgeton once belonging to Simpson & Sons. The brothers made the commercial enterprise the largest of its kind in Scotland. As part of a royal visit to Glasgow in 1859 the Prince of Wales, encouraged by his father to learn about industry, was shown round two

manufacturing companies, one being J.& J.W. Scott's in John Street, Bridgeton, the other being the Thornliebank printworks of Walter Crum.

From 1846 to 1855 he was an elected city councillor, the last four years as city treasurer. In his short time on the council he despaired of its timidity and lack of vision. He also became deputy chairman of the Clyde River Trust and convenor of its Committee on New Works. He was also a director of the Government School of Design, known later as Glasgow School of Art. His decision making was prompt and effective.

With some others he led the inception of the Loch Katrine water supply and oversaw the formation of public parks, museums and galleries of art. The formation of Kelvingrove Park was due to him. The council hesitated about buying any land for a West End park so much so that Scott stepped in and bought the land himself until the council finally saw the advantage to the public.

James Scott's greatest public attention was on improving the Clyde and anticipating the increase in size of modern ships and cargoes on a vast scale, and the importance to the commercial life of Glasgow of railway networks for the future. In his time the Clyde Trust approved major engineering work including the deepening of the Clyde and the construction of more quays and docks.

He returned to business in James Black & Co in 1856, restoring its profitability after his brother-in-law Thomas L Paterson, a new partner, let it drift despite devising technical improvements. The same Paterson had been a speculator in banks, railways, sugar and cotton and now turned to housing developments starting in Bridgeton and Ibrox before going spectacularly bankrupt, and then destitute, in his development of Dowanhill, near Great Western Road.

Improving education

The building contractor of Scott's first property in Bothwell Street, at the corner of Hope Street, in 1851 was William York who was also a respected builder of schools and bridges including Victoria Bridge. He had been a foreman in the firm of Gavin Lindsay who built for William Harley. In 1847 York constructed the school in Elmbank Street, adjacent to Bothwell Street, for the newly formed Glasgow Academy of which James Scott was a director. The leading promoter for such a school was William Campbell of Tullichewan, head of J.&W. Campbell, wholesale drapers and city warehousemen.

By the late 1860s his daughter-in-law Mrs Jessie Campbell and Mrs Jane Scott were advocating improved education for women, and gaining support from university lecturers. In 1877 Jessie Campbell and Jane Scott formed the Glasgow Association for the Higher Education of Women, resulting in the creation of Queen Margaret College, of which both ladies were founder vice-presidents. HRH Princess Louise was the president. This was the first college for women in Scotland. It would become part of Glasgow University.

The new oil industry

James Scott took a great interest in the new oil industry, and its many by-products, made possible by the methods of distilling paraffin (kerosene) from coal and oil shales patented by chemical engineer Dr James 'Paraffin' Young. He had started life as a cabinetmaker in Glasgow.

Dr James 'Paraffin' Young.

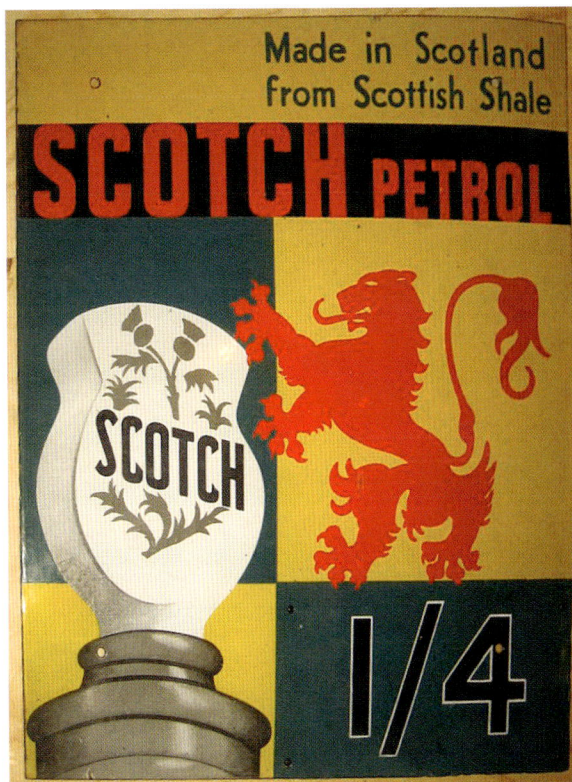

Scotch Petrol advertisement.

Scotland became the largest producer of refined oil in the world. In 1871, at age 60, Scott created the Clippens Oil Company which soon produced over 450,000 gallons of oil each month at its works in Clippens near Johnstone. It became the second largest oil company in Britain, the largest being Young's at Addiewell. He also established the Pentland Oil Company in West Lothian where most of the new oil works were based.

James Scott passed on in 1884, his wife Jane continuing until 1917.

By a sheer (and happy) coincidence a coachman of James Scott in Glasgow and Kelly was Robert Kerr, an ancestor of the author. The next generation, Stewarts through his daughter Agnes Kerr and husband Louis Stewart, became iron turners in Glasgow, and the following generation became chief engineers, captains and directors of the Frank C Strick shipping line. Strick joined with Burmah Oil of Glasgow in financing a new company to drill for oil and operate in Persia. This was the Anglo-Persian Oil Company, known today as British Petroleum. The Strick Line focussed on shipping oil from the Persian Gulf to Britain. One of their destinations here was Grangemouth with its oil refinery newly built by Scottish Oils Ltd by government order. Scottish Oils Ltd was the combination of the shale oil companies, whose engineers and expertise proved core to the Anglo-Persian Oil Company.

Chapter 18

Bothwell Street

Sulman's 1864 Bird's Eye View of Glasgow highlights Bothwell Street in the lower half. The grassed square next to Hope Street was a popular site for circuses. It held the unfulfilled dreams of railway companies.

Bothwell Street is the premier street – and widest – in Blythswood Holm, running across the southern slopes of Blythswood Hill.

With townhouses now taking up much of St Vincent Street, the Campbells of Blythswood in 1819 began promoting the sale of more of their vast lands 'to be agreeably laid out as the extension of Blythswood New Town.' By 1820 the first steading sold for building was on the north side of the proposed Bothwell Street, next to Hope Street.

The partnership buying this was the engraver and stationer James Lumsden and merchant James Smith of Jordanhill, a geographer and Arctic explorer. Both were leading supporters of the Edinburgh and Glasgow Railway Company, later known as the North British, with its small Dundas Street Station (Queen Street) opening in 1842. Lumsden would become Lord Provost, chairman and treasurer of the Royal Infirmary and founder of the Clydesdale Bank. He also became chairman of the Clyde River Trust.

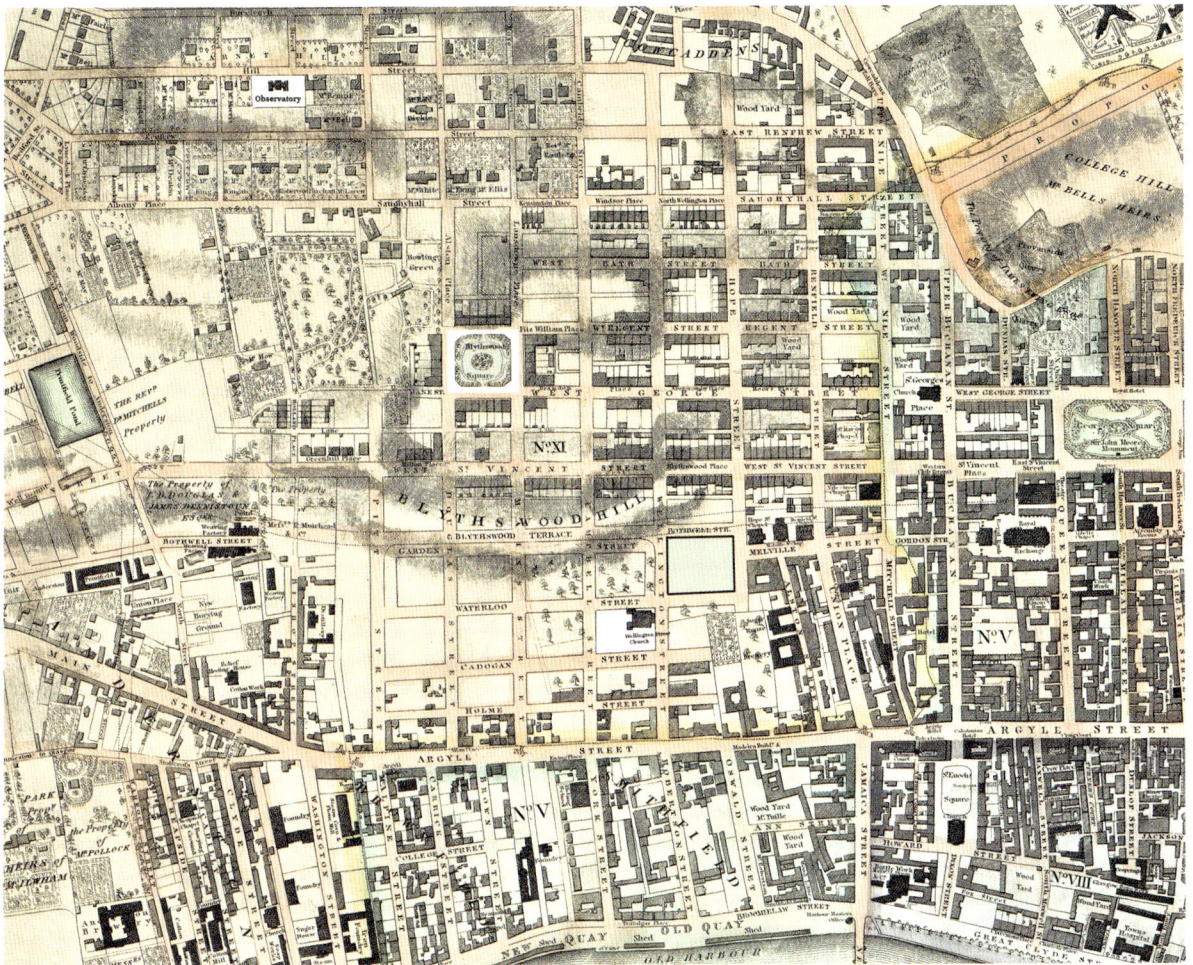

David Smith map of 1828 centred on Blythswood Hill and Square, and showing Wellington Church on its own at the corner of Waterloo Street.

Clydesdale Bank £20 note of the 21st century. The Clydesdale Bank (Virgin Money) head offices are now in Bothwell Street.

Wellington Street Church photographed in the late 1850s, and viewing along Waterloo Street.

But nothing happened in Bothwell Street for almost thirty years until calico printer and future oil pioneer James Scott of Kelly came along. In 1899 historian and printer Andrew Aird recalls his own childhood, and on Bothwell Street:

> When laid off for building purposes, the level was raised to meet the requirements of Bothwell Circus, where it joins St. Vincent Street. Many a happy day have I spent playing in and around these empty building stances, now freighted with towering and handsome piles of masonry. This street bids fair to out-rival architecturally any of our best streets.

Anderston thrives and Blythswood Holm waits

Blythswood Holm did not attract housebuilders to any extent. This was due to the slow recovery from the Napoleonic wars and to the current supply of new townhouses and terraces up the Hill. Areas further west such as Woodside and Claremont also began to attract builders. Newly-formed railway companies competed for Blythswood Holm, looking for through-routes and grand station sites. Land prices would soar.

The burgh of Anderston, with its mills and dye-works, sat lower than the Campbells' New Town extension. Blythswood Square stood even higher above Anderston, looking over the ravine carrying the Willow Bank spring waters down to the Clyde.

In David Smith's 1828 map of Glasgow, Blythswood Hill is seen in the centre and below it is the expected layout of Blythswood Holm. Only Wellington Street Church is shown as built, at the corner of Waterloo Street.

Nobody quite knew how to fully connect Blythswood and Anderston. In the meantime Anderston grew with new industries such as iron-founding, engineering and shipbuilding. One of its principal streets running north from Main Street (later renamed Argyle Street) was Bishop Street, again much lower than the edges of Blythswood Holm. A country lane, named Lang Road, stretching north to the future St George's Road, was widened and named North Street. Today it survives, partnered by the canyon of the M8 motorway.

In time the planned streets named Bothwell, Waterloo and Cadogan became centres of commerce. The Bothwell Street area became famed for shipping, oil and thread, all on a global scale. Waterloo Street and around attracted grain stores, food companies, distillers and the Corn Exchange. Cadogan Street and streets nearby became one of the centres of Glasgow's printing industry – producing commercial stationery, bank notes, books and newspapers.

The first new building and Zion Hill

Wellington Street, at the corner of Waterloo Street, saw the first new building on Blythswood Holm in 1827. This was Wellington Street Church designed by John Baird, one of the city's leading architects. The congregation previously met in Cheapside Street, Anderston, where one of the members married there was Henry Bell, future inventor of the *PS Comet*. For some twenty years Wellington Street Church stood in splendid isolation. Newspapers commented that it 'was close to but well west of the city centre, with forbidding approaches across fields, but a good road from Argyle Street'.

But eventually new warehouses, tenements and other churches were added. In the 1880s as members migrated even further west the Wellington congregation moved to a new site, today's stately Wellington Church in University Avenue.

Blythswood Holm around Waterloo Street became known as 'Zion Hill' with so many

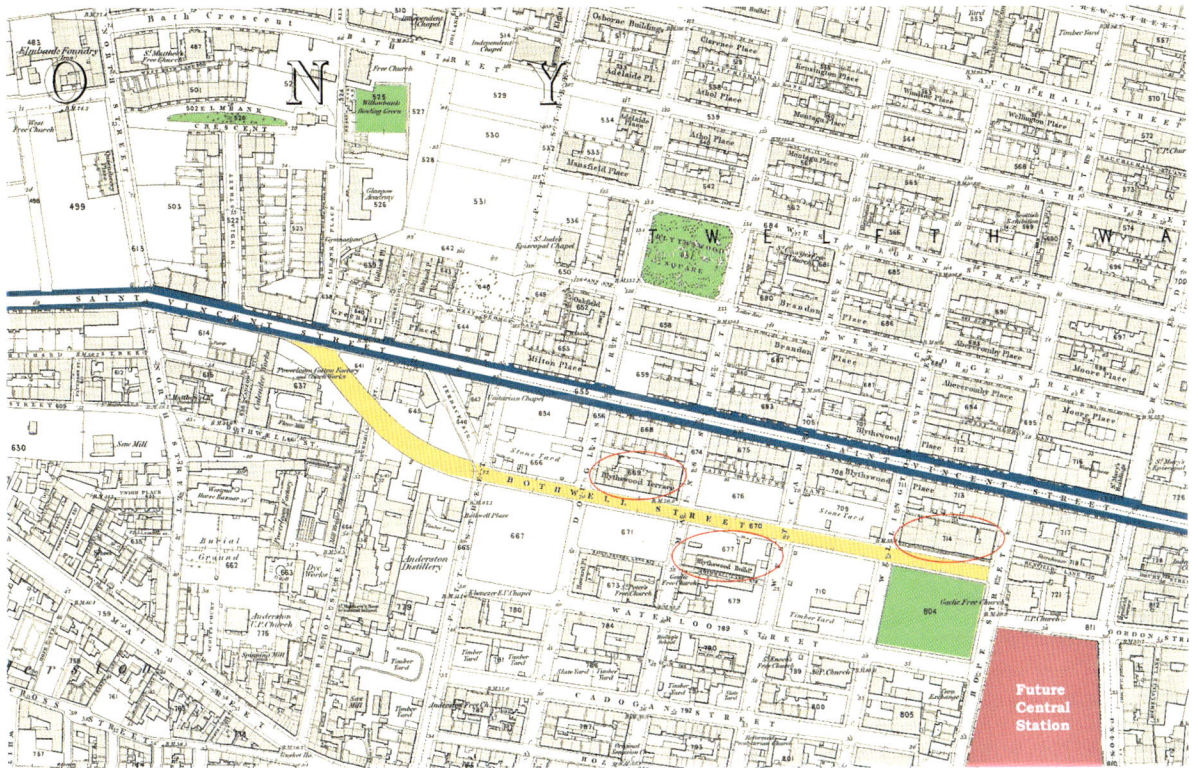

Ordnance Survey map of 1857 centred on Bothwell Street shown here in yellow, its first three buildings are circled in red.

Tram on Bothwell Circus, with Bishop Street below, approaching St Vincent Street, about 1960.

churches opening by the 1850s. The first Sabbath omnibus service in Glasgow started in 1856 when residents in Partick wanted to travel to their churches in this area. The coaches would terminate at York Street and wait for the return trip, giving time for the drivers and passengers to attend the services.

James Scott of Kelly
James Scott arrived on the scene, newly married and comfortable in business. In 1844 he had led a syndicate which bought Stobcross estate with its lands fronting the Clyde and its village of Finnieston just west of Anderston. He would soon develop one of the first crescents in Glasgow, St Vincent Crescent.

In the 1840s Scott bought most of the land on both sides of Bothwell Street. Successfully and at his own expense, he set about obtaining an Act of Parliament in 1849 to build a bridge at the western end of Bothwell Street. This would let traffic avoid Blythswood Hill's steep slopes (unfriendly to horse-power) and, instead, connect smoothly with St Vincent Street and the new suburbs beyond. A temporary connection was made by building the short, angular Terrace Street.

The bridge was a nine-arch viaduct over Bishop Street. James Scott paid for the construction of the bridge and road which opened in 1856. The new, graceful curve was named Bothwell Circus,

Arcades of the Palais-Royal, Paris.

with the *Glasgow Herald* noting: 'Bothwell Street is likely soon to become the leading thoroughfare to the West End'. It was rumoured that Edmund Glover of the Theatre Royal would raise a new theatre nearby 'out of respect to the wants of the citizens residing in the West End'.

Railway mania continued. For a new city-centre station, and leave behind its small foothold near George Square, the Edinburgh & Glasgow Railway Company in 1845 bought the large square of five Scotch acres bordered by Hope Street, Bothwell Street, Wellington Street and Waterloo Street. This was possibly from Scott or his associates. For these five acres of virgin land the company paid an enormous amount. It was half as much again as William Harley paid the Campbells for all his thirty-five acres in the 1800s.

The railway company and its ally, the Glasgow Paisley Kilmarnock & Ayrshire Railway Company, planned to run through-services north and south of the Clyde – and east and west – with a grand West Junction Terminal on Blythswood Holm. Trains would arrive from the southside to Blythswood Holm and then go by tunnel under Wellington Street to the Edinburgh line. But the Admiralty refused to let them build a bridge over the river. At the end of 1849, the whole site was sold to James Scott, at half the inflated price the railway company paid!

A visit to the Continent

With only one exception, all the first buildings in Bothwell Street were designed by Alexander Kirkland, the architect and civil engineer to James Scott. However, another equally stylish project which would have filled the five-acre Blythswood Holm square was not built, possibly because Scott got wind that more railway companies may (and did in the 1860s) wish to use it with its major vantage point at Hope Street looking along Gordon Street.

Scott and Kirkland, fresh from designing St Vincent Crescent, visited the Continent to consider what styling of buildings there might also reflect Glasgow's growth and international importance. Back in Glasgow, their plans were disclosed in 1850. Blythswood Holm at Bothwell Street would house a complex similar to Paris's Palais-Royal Arcades. Stretching from Hope Street to Wellington Street the proposed square 'of magnificent buildings to be adapted for merchants' offices, counting-houses, shops etc' would have arcades running through it. The central arcade would be thirty feet wide, flanked by two other arcades each fifteen feet wide. It is thought there would be a promenade above the colonnades, similar to the Palais-Royal. Dean of Guild Court consent was granted to build. In the event, and from the same designer, it was the north side of Bothwell Street in 1851 which first conveyed the elegance of the new street.

Bothwell Street's first buildings

Bothwell Buildings, starting at the corner of Hope Street and stretching to West Campbell Street, is the first new building of five all opening in the 1850s. Designed by Kirkland in classical style similar to the Palais-Royal, it is thought to be the first purpose-built offices in the city, apart from banks, and certainly the first building in Glasgow to be comprehensively glazed with plate-glass.

The Hope Street corner was exclusively reserved for offices while parts of the range included warehouse showrooms with full-height internal plate-glass separating the front and back saloons. Large glass domes, a feature of Kirkland's work, illuminated the rear saloons. The complete range also had fluted Corinthian columns inside.

The offices' first occupants included James Scott, who would soon add oil-refining to his portfolio. Next door were his in-laws Galbraith & Company, textile manufacturers. Alexander Kirkland also had his offices and architectural studio. One of the first showrooms promoted the domestic ironmongery of Elmbank Foundry. Shipbrokers and shipowners Patrick Henderson & Co took offices, soon to extend their services to Burma and New Zealand. Ship-owner David Hutcheson set up office to control his fleet of steamers serving the Western Highlands and Islands. Joining him was young David MacBrayne and, eventually as business and the fleet size grew, the firm now named David MacBrayne & Company moved into larger new premises just around the corner in Hope Street. The kindly biblical rhyme was very justified: 'Unto the Lord belongs the Earth/And all that it contains/Except the Kyles and Western Isles/For they belong to MacBraynes.'

Of the warehouse showrooms, no. 10 Bothwell Street was occupied by merchant W.B. Huggins from America. One of his clerks was Pierre L'Angelier, fated lover of Madeleine Smith. The 1850s were exciting.

Bothwell Buildings/Chambers, to Hope Street. Its western end was replaced by the Commercial Bank of Scotland, 1930s.

Bothwell Street about 1900. On right, Bothwell Buildings/ Chambers, Central Agency, Christian Institute buildings, Blythswood Terrace.

A travel poster of David MacBrayne Ltd.

David Carlaw & Sons' car showroom, 18 Bothwell Chambers.

Alexander Reid, portrait by Vincent van Gogh, on display in Kelvingrove Art Gallery and Museum.

Blythswood Terrace, much further west on the north side, filled the block from Blythswood Street to Douglas Street. This was a tenement of houses each of four rooms, with shops on the ground floor, built in 1851 and owned by valuator Thomas Binnie. The Binnie family created numerous spacious houses in Laurieston and in Monteith Row. The tenement continued into the 1960s when it gave way to new office headquarters for Colvilles Steel, followed by the Scottish Development Agency. Born to one of the first families in Blythswood Terrace, a young Alexander Reid grew up here to become one of the leading art dealers in Paris, London and Glasgow. He was a confidante of Van Gogh, and sometimes referred to as Van Gogh's twin.

Bothwell Street, viewing east to Hope Street from Blythswood Terrace on left, and car showrooms on right, 1961.

Eagle Buildings on south side of Bothwell Circus at the corner of Pitt Street.

Blythswood Buildings, a furnishings warehouse set back on the south side at 85 Bothwell Street, was designed by Alexander Kirkland and opened in 1854. This expanding emporium selling household ironmongery and travel equipment was run by James Allan of Elmbank Foundry. In true Kirkland style there was a long Italianate arcade from the street to the main building. Allan's Elmbank Foundry was on the west side of North Street looking over to Bath Crescent. In the 1900s the foundry was demolished and the Mitchell Library built on its site.

In 1859 two more buildings emerged, both owned by James Scott and designed by Kirkland. On the south side at Pitt Street, the **Eagle Buildings** in Venetian style, containing warehouses and showrooms, stretched in a concave curve following Bothwell Circus.

Bothwell Street, viewing over to the Christian Institute buildings in 1919.

In Parisian style on the north side of Bothwell Circus the very tall, curving **Bothwell Circus Buildings** with their offices, manufacturing warehouses and showrooms graced the junction with St Vincent Street, wrapping round and in to the short Terrace Street behind it.

A few years later Alexander Kirkland and his family emigrated to America where he would become the Commissioner of Public Buildings for Chicago.

Divine fabric

Vacant steadings, often complete blocks of land from one street to the next, remained a feature. These were used as stone-yards and timber-yards by contractors. In the twentieth century, especially at the western end, some became car showrooms and garages. But in the 1880s and 90s substantial buildings took up position.

The **Christian Institute**, designed in German Renaissance style by architect John McLeod, took pride of place in 1879 in the centre of the north block between West Campbell Street and Blythswood Street. McLeod was also the architect of Garnethill Synagogue. The institute's halls and rooms became well used by numerous organisations, including the annual Glasgow Schools Music Festival.

The Central Agency building in Bothwell Street.

Early advertising of cotton threads of J&P Coats.

In the 1890s two major buildings in matching Gothic style were added next to the institute, both designed by architect Robert A Bryden. He also designed much of Quarrier's Homes in Bridge of Weir. On the east side, the Bible Training Institute opened with its one hundred bedrooms for male students, fifty bedrooms for female students; and with libraries, sitting rooms, writing rooms and dining rooms for each sex. The education and training was the equal of Trinity College near Park Circus. In 1917/19 the **Bible Training Institute** became the American YMCA to help serve the thousands of American soldiers arriving in the city.

The equally immense **YMCA** hotel opened on the block's west side with 195 bedrooms, club sitting rooms, gymnasium and restaurant – all open to the public. The Young Men's Christian Association had five major buildings in the city, one in each of the north, south, west and east districts and the central one in Bothwell Street.

Red sandstone now became the building material of choice (and need) because white sandstone quarries were being exhausted.

The Central Agency building, continuing today at 50 Bothwell Street, is the grandest and most important of the first red sandstoned offices. The *Glasgow Herald* reports in 1891: 'The buildings are to be in the Elizabethan and Greek style of architecture, and constructed in red stone, with polished granite pillars extending to the first floor.' The entire stonework is exquisitely carved, including masks representing different nations and subtle profile heads of Athena, the Greek goddess of wisdom and associated with handicrafts,

spinning and weaving, and of Mercury, the Roman god of commerce and communications.

Designed by architect David Barclay, and built by Morrison & Mason, it was erected in stages in the 1890s on the north side between Wellington Street and West Campbell street. This was the nerve centre of the worldwide marketing and selling of threads. J&P Coats had become the 'pioneering manufacturing multinational.'

The Central Agency was formed in 1889 by the cotton sewing thread manufacturers J&P Coats

The Central Chambers on Blythswood Holm at Hope Street and Bothwell Street.

Architect's drawing of the Central Chambers, Hope Street façade, 1877.

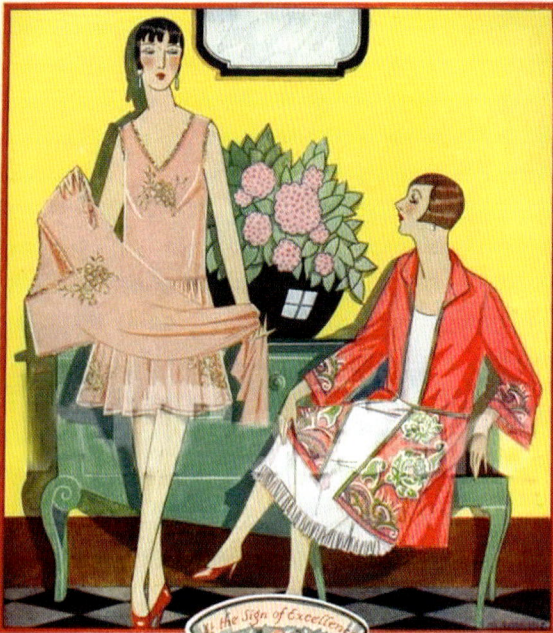

J&P Coats and Clark & Co advertising in *The Needlewoman* magazine, 1920.

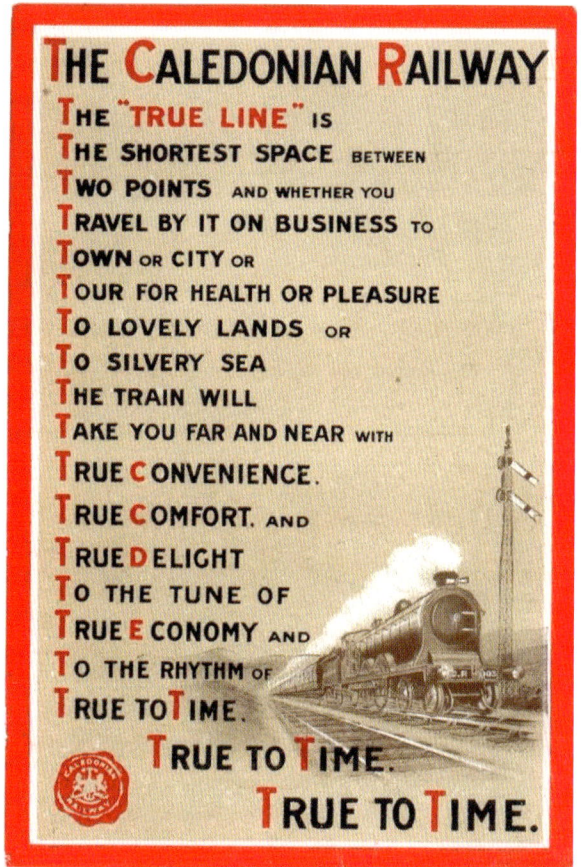

One of the True Line poster series of the Caledonian Railway company.

of Paisley and their neighbours, and rivals of equal prominence, Clark & Co. Some other cotton thread makers in Britain came on board as did Lister & Co's silk threads. By 1900, The Central Agency was responsible for sales in 150 different countries in thirty different currencies. The manufacturers shared the representatives and costs in each country apart from the USA which had its own arrangements for the Coats and Clark mills there.

Coats and Clark soon merged, but kept their identities separate when selling world-wide.

J&P Coats Ltd in size and profits was the equal of Standard Oil or of US Steel, and by far the largest company in Britain. They added more offices directly behind their Bothwell Street premises in St Vincent Street, joining the buildings by an enclosed bridge over St Vincent Lane. In time St Vincent Street housed the headquarter offices of the Coats Paton combine.

The Caledonian Railway steams in

By the early 1860s the Caledonian Railway Company induced James Scott to sell to them his **Blythswood Holm** square of five acres next to

Hope Street, and the lengths along the south of Bothwell Street to Pitt Street. He kindly accepted the financial profit!

The mighty Caledonian proposed in 1865 to have railway lines from Renfrewshire and Ayrshire come into a new planned (but unbuilt) city-centre station between Pitt Street and Hope Street. This would be by tunnelling under the Clyde near Whiteinch, first arriving at Partick and then proceeding to Bothwell Street. Passing east out of the new central-station, lines would be underground via George Street to High Street and from there above ground to Lanarkshire, and on to Edinburgh and London.

By the 1870s it was thought that a railway bridge directly over the Clyde from Eglinton Street would gain planning permission, and so it did, with a struggle. Blythswood Holm's square would become the grand central terminus. Buying more land on the west side of Hope Street down to the Clyde proved to be very costly. Instead, the railway company bought the cheaper land to the east of Hope Street where the old district of Grahamston survived.

Central Station in its early size was up and running on Hope Street's east side by 1880. There was no hotel at this stage. A speculative property company, with its Edinburgh architects Peddie & Kinnear, bought half of the square fronting Hope Street and sweeping into Bothwell Street and Waterloo Street.

The result, appearing around 1880, was the imposing French-style **Central Chambers** continuing today with entrances from the three streets. Designed as a hotel with 130 rooms, shops on the ground floor and a planned arcade behind it, the owners assumed (very wrongly)

that the railway company would be interested in taking it over. The promoters even named it the 'Caledonian Central Hotel' and advertised for an operator. However, there was never an agreement at any time with the Caledonian for passenger use.

The hotel-that-never-was quickly shut. Above the ground floor all the levels were changed to offices. Even today the higher floors resemble long hotel corridors with rooms off each side.

The Caledonian Railway's Central Station was greatly enlarged in the later 1880s, and onwards, including the addition of its masterly 400-bedroom Central Hotel at the corner of Gordon Street.

Chapter 19

West to St Vincent Crescent

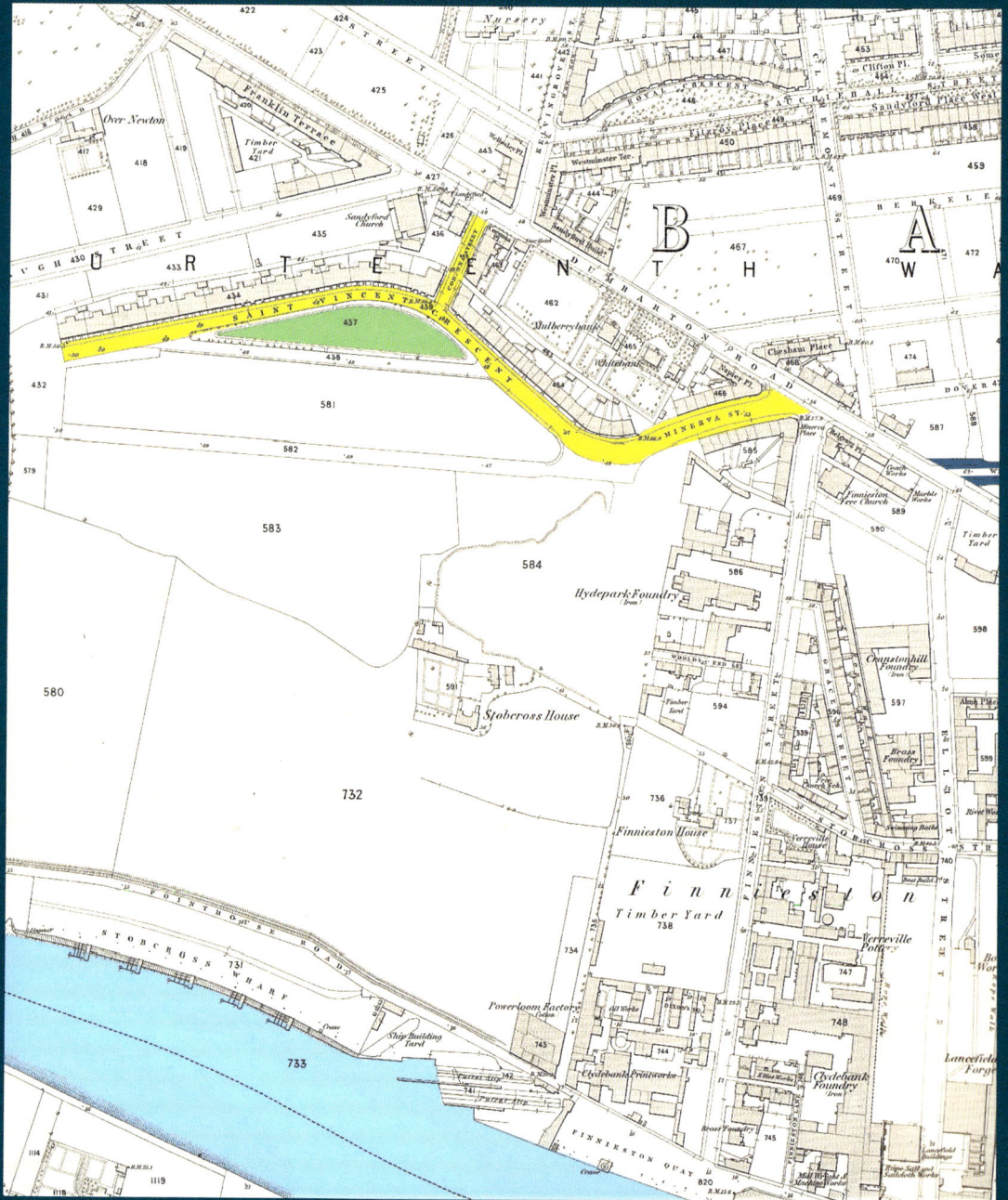

Ordnance Survey map of 1857 highlighting St Vincent Crescent and Minerva Street on the northern edges of Stobcross Estate, with West St Vincent Street arriving on the right.

With his vision for city improvements and the need for more land to expand Glasgow Harbour, James Scott led a syndicate of investors which in 1844 bought Stobcross mansion-house and estate, to the west of Anderston. Its total of 80 imperial acres was bounded by the Clyde and rose north to Dumbarton Road, then named as Main Street, Anderston.

As pre-arranged he sold 35 acres of it to the Clyde River Trust. Finnieston Street was on its east side and Yorkhill to its west. The sale proceeds from the Trust more than covered the full cost of buying the complete estate!

The syndicate, later known as the Stobcross Proprietors, started parcelling areas for housing. James Scott and his architect Alexander Kirkland devised the most splendid of developments, obtaining Dean of Guild Court consent in 1849. This is the long serpentine creation of St Vincent Crescent with seventy houses, its short Corunna Street linking to Dumbarton Road, and the equally gracious Minerva Street curving on to Dumbarton Road at the top of Finnieston Street. One hundred yards away, West St Vincent Street

Stobcross House and lands, facing the Clyde, 18th century painting.

emerged past Thomas Hopkirk's former Botanic Gardens at Sandyford.

At the same time they were developing Bothwell Street, connecting to St Vincent Street.

St Vincent Crescent
In 1851, Senex writes:

> The Stobcross lands have now been laid out with streets, terraces and crescents, underlaid with splendid common sewers, and shaped into a beautiful crescent. In front of the crescent two acres, enclosed with a highly ornamental railing, have been laid out as pleasure-grounds for the tenants. The architectural style is Italianate; the height of the houses three storeys; and they are let in flats, varying each from ten rooms and kitchen to five rooms and kitchen, with of course all the modern improvements. The rents of these fine middle-class dwellings range from £70 to £40 each, a year.

The selling agents state: 'The Property is most desirable as a residence, having a most commanding view of upwards of ten miles of fine open country'. Advertisements declare the tenements: ' have been erected in a most substantial manner, with all modern improvements, and have been Painted and Papered; the windows furnished with Venetian Blinds, and the whole finished in a superior style'. Each house 'has Plunge and Shower Baths, Washing House, excellent Bleaching Green, and etc'.

As new houses were completed over the next few years the newspapers still marvelled at

St Vincent Crescent and its bowling greens, 1862.

St Vincent Crescent in full bloom today.

Minerva Street at Finnieston wending down to the start of St Vincent Crescent.

the comprehensive planning: 'including the extensive green lawn in the centre, in which residenters may take exercise and enjoy (as they have already done) archery contests and other sports on summer evenings'. To the south of the pleasure-gardens it was intended to build another terrace, but was not.

With the band of the 2nd Northern Battalion of Rifle Volunteers in full tune 'while the coloured uniforms of representatives from the Engineer, Celtic, and other Rifle Companies gave an appearance of gaiety and variety to the grounds', the first bowling green was opened in 1860. This was the start of St Vincent Bowling Club. James Scott of Kelly accepted the post of honorary president. A large pond with a decorative fountain in the middle was also declared open, to be used in the winter for curling on four rinks. That curling pond was replaced in 1876 by an ash court for the newly-formed Crescent Tennis Club. To the south of the pleasure gardens the very large area earmarked for another terrace was made into St Vincent Pond, complete with boating.

Responding to public demands, St Vincent Crescent was defined as a Conservation Area in 1975.

Glasgow Harbour with Queen's Dock centre left and Yorkhill Quay before it, on right is Princes Dock.

Queen's Dock

James Scott was also deputy chairman of the Clyde River Trust and chairman of its Board of Works. Its engineers drew up outline plans for a tidal dock in 1845 onwards. It was the 1860s when fuller plans emerged for a larger set of docks.

The syndicate sold 20 acres of the Stobcross lands in 1864 to the North British Railway Company for them to open a Stobcross Goods Station and through-routes. Again, the proceeds were more than the original cost of the whole estate. It was all profit!

The North British built their mineral goods depot close to Finnieston Street, and extensive sidings mainly for coaling and timber, having first built an engine shed and turntables. The Caledonian built their mineral goods depot just south of it, while sharing the tracks. Construction of the railways and of the docks took place in the late 1870s.

Queen's Dock, named by royal permission, was fully completed in 1880 at which time it was the largest in Scotland and the fourth largest in Britain.

The extensive Queen's Dock now embraced thirty-four acres of quays and water and full facilities for trade. Ships sailing from it included those of the Hutchison Line, Burrell & Son, Paddy Henderson, Donaldson Line, Clan Line and City Line. From 1904 the new Yorkhill Quay built next to the dock entrance accommodated the Anchor Line and the Blue Funnel Line.

Queen's Dock, south basin, 1907, painting by John Young Hunter.

When shipping finished at Queen's Dock ninety years later, the entire site was bought by the Scottish Development Agency who infilled it and created the Scottish Exhibition and Conference Centre with the Forum Hotel adjacent and room for more buildings to follow. Today the docks contain the Scottish Exhibition Centre, the Clyde Auditorium (a mighty armadillo), the Hydro Arena and numerous hotels.

Queen's Dock today, containing the Scottish Exhibition campus. St Vincent Crescent and its bowling greens on the left.

Chapter 20

Elmbank Crescent and Its Cousins

Upper staircases and landings of Scottish Opera, Elmbank Crescent.

Just west of William Harley's Willow Bank, owners of some mansions and grounds decided they too might make money by building streets and houses.

The first to be sold was the picturesque Napiershall with its long driveway at the top of Bishop Street, Anderston. This had been owned by Thomas Napier whose family also owned land further north at Great Western Road. Thomas Napier was a watchmaker. His fine watches and the longcase clocks of his former apprentices are collected today.

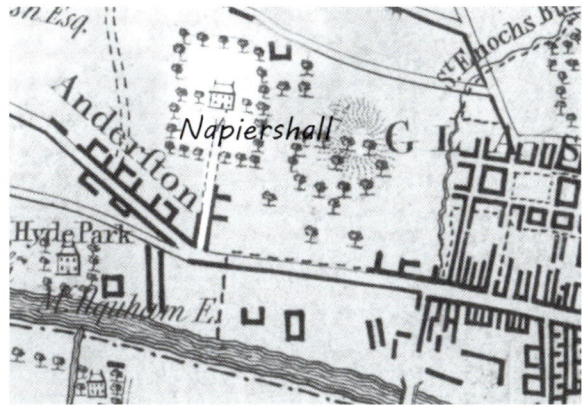

Thomas Richardson's map of 1795 detailing Napiershall, north of Anderston.

On the passing of his daughter, the venerable Miss Napier, in 1809, Napiershall was bought by merchants from Anderston who renamed it Greenhill. William Robertson, a builder and councillor in Anderston, built houses in Greenhill Place (later part of St Vincent Street), then opened and built Holland Place (the start of Holland Street) and likewise Elm Bank Place (much later named Elmbank Street). He would become the builder of much of India Street leading to Elmbank Crescent.

open Glasgow Academy, on the east side of Elm Bank Place.

Adjacent to Howe's property was the mansion and extensive gardens of the Macnair family. William Macnair led the way on the boldest development that was close to Blythswood Square, namely the creation of Elmbank Crescent and its gardens and India Street. The master-plan was devised by an architect from Edinburgh, Patrick Wilson.

Next to Napiershall was the mansion and grounds of James How(e), whose country house was the Grange, near Kilmarnock. He was a foreign hide merchant, based much of the time in Bahia, Brazil, and trading with his brothers in Glasgow. In the 1840s a large part of his land was sold to the committee who would build and

Gold repousse watch by Thomas Napier.

Silver watch by Thomas Napier, about 1760.

Longcase clock by Daniel Brown, about 1775, onetime Napier apprentice.

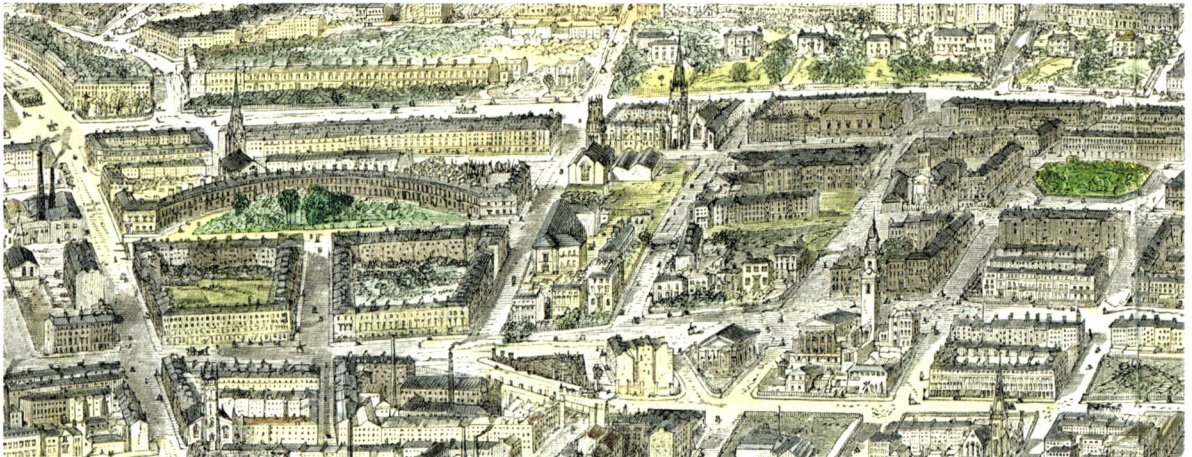

Sulman's 1864 Bird's Eye View of Glasgow, with Elmbank Crescent and its gardens, India Street and Elmbank Street centre left. Beyond is Sauchiehall Street, westward to Charing Cross.

South side of Elmbank Crescent from India Street, beyond is Elmbank Street.

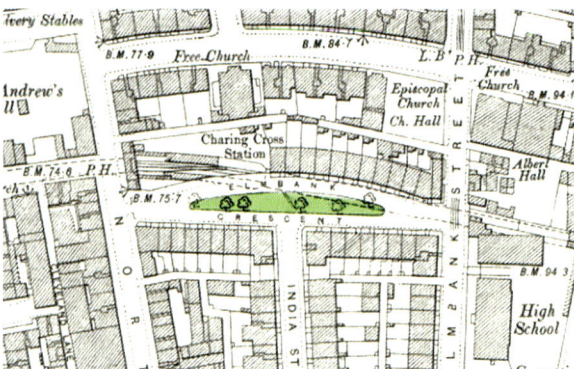

Elmbank Crescent and its gardens, showing the first impact of Charing Cross station from 1886.

BEAUTIFUL CRESCENT

BUILDING GROUND FOR SALE OR FEUING

AT THE WEST END OF GLASGOW

A FEW STEADINGS on the Line of that well-known and beautiful Crescent, called ELMBANK CRESCENT, are still for Sale.

Its situation is in the near neighbourhood of St Vincent Street, and between the Sauchy-hall road (on the projected line of Regent Street).

A great part of this Crescent is already built and occupied. The architecture is chaste, but plain and elegant, and has been greatly admired. Single Steadings may be had, or more, as desired. Apply to Mr MACNAIR, No. 12, Gordon Street: or No.16, of the Crescent, Glasgow: or here to Mr PATRICK WILSON, architect, 15, St. Andrew Square.

Advertising in *The Scotsman*, 10th November, 1838.

Elmbank Crescent and gardens

The Macnair mansion 'off the Saughy-hall road' was owned by William Macnair. His father had been a bookbinder and bookseller in Saltmarket and his mother was a daughter of the Duncan family who became printers to Glasgow University. Macnair continued the family interest in fine art and books. In the 1820s and 30s he was the accountant and notary public (lawyer) to the well-established Thistle Bank based in Virginia Street. After more than seventy years in business it merged in 1836 with the Glasgow Union Bank. At this point William McNair struck out on his own as an accountant and agent.

To develop his own property he appointed Patrick Wilson as architect. This was shortly after Wilson had redesigned and rebuilt Caprington Castle, near Kilmarnock, in palatial baronial style for Sir William Cunninghame and family. The construction of Elmbank Crescent was underway by the late 1830s. Patrick Wilson enthused about crescents, and later gave talks about the early development of Edinburgh New Town. He designed Dalmellington Parish Church in the 1840s for Henry Houldsworth of Anderston, who was diversifying from cotton spinning to iron and coal. In 1850 Wilson became a founding member, and later chairman, of the Architectural Institute of Scotland.

The self-contained houses, with shrubbery in front of the whole crescent, sold for around £1,750 each, 'consisting of a Sunk Storey with Sunk Area in front, Ground Storey, and Upper Storey':

> The Ground and Upper Flats contain Dining-Room. Drawing-Room, Parlour, Ante-Room. Pantry, Store-Room, and five Bed-Rooms, Bath-Room, etc. The Sunk Flat contains Kitchen, Laundry. Larder, Servants' Room, Washing-House. Offices, etc.

Unfortunately, William Macnair ran out of money in 1844, but the second half of the crescent was completed in the 1850s.

The Underground cometh

The first Underground railway in Scotland was the Glasgow City & District line, opening in 1886. It dealt a mortal blow to the western half of Elmbank Crescent.

Linking with the North British railway services from Edinburgh through to Lanarkshire, the new underground was built from High Street, underneath George Street to the new Low-Level platforms of Queen Street Station. It continued (and continues) west, tunnelling deep under West Regent Street, heading to Partick and up on to Milngavie and Helensburgh. First stop, Charing Cross!

The new station was built by cutting down from the top. It was open to the skies, to help clear smoke from 194 steam trains each full day! The amount of smoke and shortness of platforms led to complaints. Within ten years the North British bought the eastern half of the crescent curve, demolishing it and making the larger station open to the elements apart from a glass roof over each platform.

Some of the remaining houses on the south of the crescent became institutions such as the Glasgow Hospital for Women (before the Royal Samaritan Hospital for Women opened beyond Eglinton Toll), and the Glasgow Ear Nose and Throat Hospital (before moving to a new building in St Vincent Street). One property became a theatrical residential club, arranged by the YWCA and officially opened by Sybil Thorndike. In later decades two regimental clubs opened. And a kosher hotel run by Bessie Shinwell was open to all, but serving only kosher food.

India Street, the hotel and the bagpipes

The residents of India Street were as prosperous as Elmbank Crescent's and the houses were of similar size, usually four public rooms and five bedrooms. In the 1850s architect James Smith and his family settled in India Street before moving up to Blythswood Square. Daughter Madeleine started her liaison with the doomed Pierre, inviting him in, in India Street.

On the east side, More's Hotel, initially combining four townhouses and soon to expand, was started in 1911 by Jessie More, a wealthy widow. It was a gracious hotel and became a favourite for weddings.

Steam train arriving at Charing Cross station.

In 1926, More's Hotel had to take a new neighbour to court for disturbance to guests by the playing of bagpipes into the wee small hours of many mornings. The new neighbour was the Highlanders' Institute, just moved in to their first home at 25/29 Elmbank Street, backing on to India Street. To their club rooms in the institute they added a function hall at the back (which building continues today). During that first winter many dances and social entertainments had been held with noisy dancing and bagpipe playing. According to the settlement:

> The Institute guarantees that the dancing of Scottish reels, and the playing of bagpipes, will cease at 11 o 'clock in the evening during the coming winter; that it will deafen both exit doors in the lane adjoining the Institute; that double windows will be installed in all the windows of the dancing hall; that all windows will be kept shut; and that the programmes for dances will be previously submitted to the Institute.

Guests could now sleep. In 1961 the Highlanders' Institute moved to larger and modern premises round the corner in Berkeley Street taking over what had been Bobby Jones' Berkeley Ballroom. At this point, the former institute re-focussed as the (Rev.) Tom Allan Centre, helping people in need.

More's Hotel continued to the 1970s, being replaced by office blocks for the newly-formed Strathclyde Regional Council.

More's Hotel on the east side of India Street.

View north in Elmbank Street to Sauchiehall Street, and the Beresford Hotel being completed in 1938.

Offices for Strathclyde Regional Council, India Street from Elmbank Crescent. Beyond is the Hilton Hotel, William Street, Anderston.

Elmbank Street

Coming south in its new name, through the Sauchiehall Street tenements to Bath Street, Elmbank Street avoids the steeper slopes of Blythswood Hill. Tramway services, horse and then electric, linked easily to St Vincent Street and Bothwell Street, passing the former bowling club and current high school buildings on the east, and the terraces of what had been Elm Bank Place on the west.

To tens of thousands of households it seems that the Scout shop and the Girl Guide shop have been in Elmbank Street for ever.

Institution of Engineers and Shipbuilders in Scotland

On Elmbank Crescent at the corner of Elmbank Street, the Institution of Engineers and Shipbuilders opened their new building in 1907. The corner site, formerly occupied by townhouses, was available because the railway contractors had to use it to help clear away the curved crescent in the 1890s. Formed by mathematician and scientist Professor W.J. Mcquorn Rankine (a resident of St Vincent Street) and others in 1857, the Institution reflected the importance of energy, engineering and modern shipbuilding internationally. It is built of Black Pasture hard stone from Northumberland, the same quarries that the Romans used to build Hadrian's Wall.

Elmbank Street viewing across to Glasgow High school, about 1900.

In St Vincent Street, at the foot of Elmbank Street, the Guardian Royal Exchange Assurance offices were built in the 1960s, with neighbouring new offices at the foot of India Street.

Its halls, rooms and library continue today largely unchanged. From 1968 it has been occupied by Scottish Opera, close to the King's theatre where the company's first productions started from 1962 onwards under Sir Alexander Gibson.

New vistas

On the western edges of central Blythswood, after the M8 motorway cleared its way in the 1960s through Anderston and underneath Charing Cross, new vistas open from a great height – across a chasm – if you live or work in the range of high-rise offices, hotels, or flats, now in place.

Elmbank Gardens had the first multi-storey office building (now a hotel) along the new frontier. This is the white Y-ARD building, west of the King's theatre, housing the scientists and engineers of Yarrows shipbuilding company and the Admiralty involved in researching and developing new propulsion and weaponry for naval ships. There was also a unit responsible for the maintenance of the Royal Yacht Britannia, and the planning and control of its voyages around the world.

Among other multi-storeys now thronging the western ends of Bothwell Street and St Vincent Street, the new white buildings of Scottish Power, at the foot of Elmbank Street and what was India Street, enjoy views over every point of the compass. Its staff can see for miles including in its prospect its former Cathcart headquarters located in the landscaped grounds of the South of Scotland Electricity Board.

Close your mind to motorway sounds, to the immense growth of Glasgow in the last two centuries and you are back in 1814 when Swiss merchant Hans C. Escher was touring Britain. After meeting William Harley and being at Garnethill Observatory, his diary entry is accurate:

Above all I enjoyed the wonderful view which is better than any that I have seen so far. To the left lay Glasgow in a slight mist and to the right lay the valley of the Clyde. I could see the [High Church] Tower of Paisley, the hills crowned with wonderful groups of trees, the soft green meadows, the reapers in the cornfields. And beyond lay the hills of Dumbarton, Ben Lomond and the Highlands. Never before have I seen such a wonderful pattern of form and colour. Never before have I seen such architectural beauty in so fine a natural setting.

Elmbank Street residents, former Highlanders' Institute on left; and the Institution of Engineers & Shipbuilders in Scotland, now Scottish Opera

Architectural elevation to Elmbank Crescent of the Institution of Engineers & Shipbuilders, 1907. The sculptures proposed for the entrance and above the grand window did not proceed.

Bothwell Street.

A TO Z

Bath Street is named because of the public baths pioneered by William Harley in the 1800s, next to West Nile Street. This was one of the new ventures of Harley when he was developing Blythswood.

Its eminent position at the top of Blythswood Hill has attracted merchant princes and not a few Lord Provosts, with housing to suit. Over decades it has drawn to it, and to nearby Blythswood Square, reams of doctors and surgeons, some with consulting rooms in their residence, and others engaged in the new hospitals and clinics opening up.

Recovery and pleasure is offered by the King's Theatre, but the Albert Ballroom has gone, and the twinkling toes. The co-ordination of eye, hand and brain is hosted by the very sociable Glasgow Art Club.

See also: *Harley's Water* from page 54, *Harley's Baths in Bath Street* from page 58, *Harley's Byres and Willowbank Dairy* from page 64 and *Harley's Willowbank Baking Company* from page 72.

Left: Bath Street, westwards at Douglas Street.

Below: Townhouses in Bath Street between Blythswood Street (formerly Mains Street) and Douglas Street.

Bath Street east from Renfield Street, on the left were the baths and other ventures of William Harley, stretching to West Nile Street.

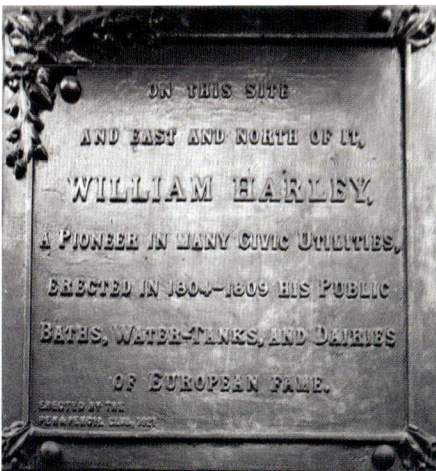

Wall plaque at the corner with Renfield Street commemorating William Harley and his Public Baths, Water-tanks and Dairies of European Fame.

Bath Street with Adelaide Place Baptist Church, the most senior of Baptist churches in Scotland, at the corner of Pitt Street.

Left: Bath Street, at Wellington Street, 1930s. The largest of the magnificent stores in Sauchiehall Street also had buildings connecting through to Bath Street. Nearest is Copland & Lye, and the others are of Pettigrew & Stephens – by the 1900s the largest store in the city.

Right: In Bath Street, past West Campbell Street, the third property along, now a hotel, was built in 1912 as Glasgow School Board's headquarters. One of the townhouses built over was that of Lord Provost Sir James Campbell, whose son Henry Campbell-Bannerman became Prime Minister.

Artist E.A. Walton and his wife at home in 203 Bath Street. The drawing-room became his studio.

ART LIFE

Following the freshness of the New Town, its housing and wealth, the art dealers and their galleries around Buchanan Street and Jamaica Street expanded across Renfield Street, West George Street and Sauchiehall Street. Over the years, the innovative dealers include Connell, Bennett, Lawrie, Reid, Angus, Annan, Honeyman, MacNicol, Hardie, Lennie, Gerber and Bilcliffe.

The art school moved up from Ingram Street to the new Corporation Galleries in Sauchiehall Street, and then Renfrew Street. Those attending the art school and practitioners out in the big world created, and sometimes shared, personal studios to suit their times. In Garnethill this was especially the case in Renfrew Street and Rose Street. Likewise, Blythswood hosted studios and clusters of studios, including Bath Street, West Regent Street, Hope Street and St Vincent Street. Those closest to galleries were sought after!

Charles Rennie Mackintosh and his wife and fellow artist Margaret Macdonald Mackintosh settled in Mains Street (later known as Blythswood Street). Their art nouveau furniture, white fitments, and designs moved with them near to the University, which today has them on permanent display. In latter decades, the colourist JD Fergusson and his wife, the revolutionary dancer Margaret Morris, had their studios in West George Street at the corner of Blythswood Square – one for painting and a studio theatre for dance. The Queen's Sculptor, Benno Schotz, worked out of Wellington Street.

At the Lady Artists' Club.

HER FRIEND - And I suppose you study Art a good deal?
THE LADY ARTIST - Art! You don't think I dare study Art.
It might spoil my style !

Above: Glasgow Art Club, entrance hall at 185 Bath Street.

Far left: Glasgow Art Club's gallery, designed by John Keppie and Charles Rennie Macintosh.

Left: Conversation at an exhibition of the Lady Artists' Club, Blythswood Square. "HER FRIEND – And I suppose you study Art a good deal? THE LADY ARTIST – Art! You don't think I dare study Art. It might spoil my style !"

Glasgow.   Bath Street.

Right: Bath Street in the 1890s, opened here as Bath Crescent from the 1850s, curving east from North Street. On the right is St Matthew's Highlanders' Memorial Church opposite Newton Street.

Below: Bath Street in the 1900s with, on the left from Holland Street, Bath Street Church opening in 1877, Albert Ballroom, Renfield Church and the King's Theatre at the corner of Elmbank Street. Beyond is the St Matthew's Highlanders' Memorial Church.

BATH ST GLASGOW

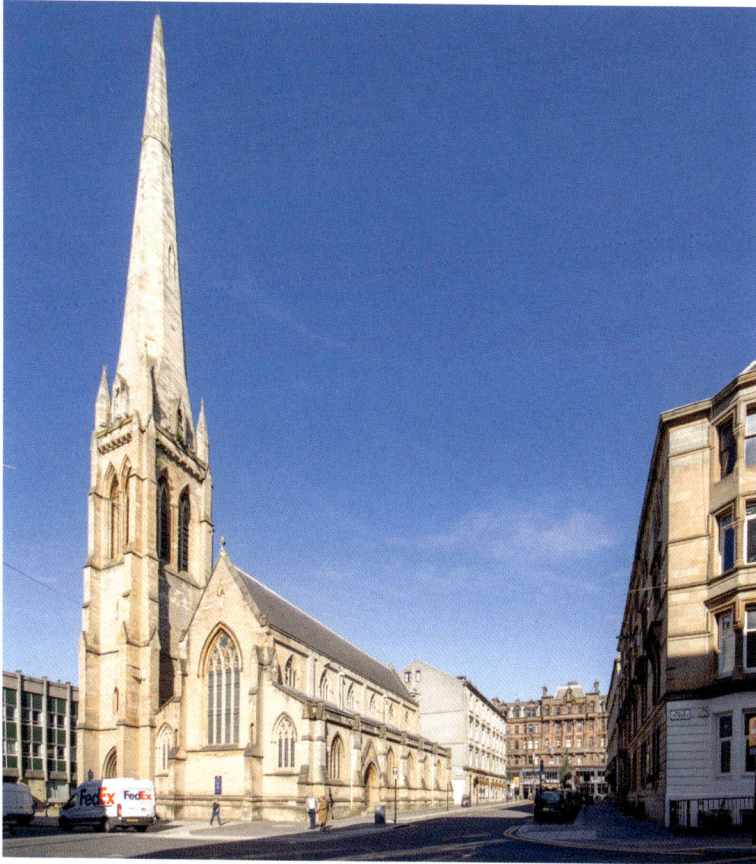

Left: Heavenly aspiration from 1852, St Matthew's Church, at Holland Street with Sauchiehall Street beyond. Later known as Renfield-St Stephen's Church and now as St Andrew's West Church. The tranquil Renfield Centre is linked to it, left.

Below: The King's Theatre on the corner of Elmbank Street opened in 1904 as part of the Howard & Wyndham group of theatres.

Right: Bath Street at Blythswood Street.

Below: Designed by John Burnet snr., Elgin Place Congregational Church opened in Bath Street in 1856 at the corner of Pitt Street – which was first named as Elgin Place. Classical and in balance with its neighbourhood.

Above: Bath Street, comfortable and on the level.

Left: Glasgow Art Club, nightshift.

BLYTHSWOOD SQUARE

Blythswood Square is William Harley's jewel in the crown. Devised by him, it was built in the 1820s. It has housed the great and the good – and some in between.

Within living memory it has housed the Lady Artists' Club. the Agricultural College before moving its rooms to Auchincruive, the Royal Scottish Automobile Club, Baillie's Institution before its reading rooms and books went to the Mitchell Library, and below it the Ambassador Restaurant, the pinnacle of many restaurants opened by Mario Romano in his adopted city.

'THE SQUARE at BLYTHSWOOD HILL is now formed. The delightful prospect, fine air, and good access, render this site peculiarly desirable as a Town and Country residence.'
William Harley

See also: *Blythswood Pleasure Gardens* from page 38, *First New Houses* from page 86, *Money Matters and the Smith Family* from page 102, *Blythswood Square* from page 106 and *Royal Scottish Automobile Club* from page 116.

Left: Sylvan view across the square from one of the townhouses.

Below: The east side of Blythswood Square in line with Blythswood Street. Formerly the Royal Scottish Automobile Club, now hotel.

LADY ARTISTS' CLUB

Started in 1882 by eight woman students of Glasgow School of Art, the Lady Artists' Club was Britain's first society of women artists, and the first residential club for women in Britain. It continued in Blythswood Square from 1893 till 1971. The club's entrance is seen below, second from the right. Its neighbour to the right became the West of Scotland Agricultural College, and to the left the townhouses became and remain offices of international companies.

Adding to its studios, tearoom and club rooms, a members' gallery was designed by George Walton, and the front entrance redesigned by Charles Rennie Macintosh in 1908.

The photograph taken inside the club shows, from back left: Dorothy Carleton Smyth, Norah Neilson Gray, Eleanor Allen Moore, Helen Paxton Brown (with parasol) and centre front is Jessie M. King.

Above: Inside the Lady Artists' Club around 1900, at 5 Blythswood Square. *Right*: The front door to the Lady Artists' Club.
Below: The north side of Blythswood Square in line with West Regent Street.

Right: West Regent Street rises up to Blythswood Square.

Below right: Starting point of the annual Monte Carlo Rally, 1961.

Below: Railings with style.

Bottom: Entrance hall of the Blythswood Square Hotel, originally designed in the 1920s for the Royal Scottish Automobile Club.

Right: The west side of Blythswood Square in line with Douglas Street.

Below: West George Street arriving at Blythswood Square.

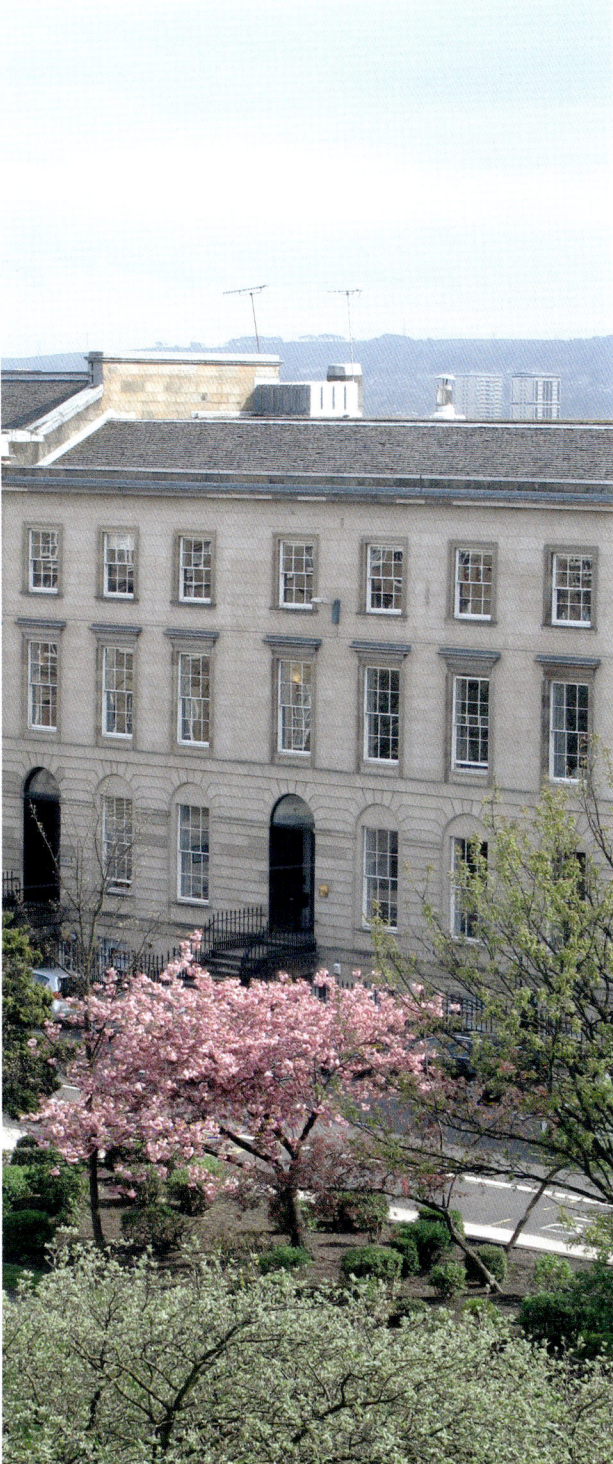

Left: View over the gardens and south side of Blythswood Square, and beyond.

BLYTHSWOOD STREET

Blythswood Street is the name given in the 1920s, a century after starting life as Mains Street.

It was in the 1920s when Glasgow's population reached 1.1 million following boundary expansions that duplicated street names were reviewed and given unique ones.

Mains Street was its name from the start of the New Town of Blythswood in the 1800s, reflecting the estate of Mains (today's Milngavie) owned for some 600 years by the Douglas family. They fell heir to the Lands of Blythswood and later required to adopt the surname of Campbell.

It is the prime link, and easiest walk, connecting Garnethill, Sauchiehall Street and Blythswood Square. Beyond are dramatic vistas at each stage of its descent to Argyle Street.

Blythswood Street arrives at Blythswood Square and continues south, down to Argyle Street.

The New Town rear gardens and coach-houses changed over time to parking, garages and property extension.

BOTHWELL STREET

Bothwell Street refers to the Lanarkshire origins of the Douglas families, in particular Bothwell whose castle was a Douglas stronghold. Anderston's earlier Bothwell Street further west was similar in line to the new street.

Bothwell Street is the premier street on Blythswood Holm. It sits well. It smiles with success. The latest of the glass towers at the western end has a running track on its roof. This'll keep staff on their toes.

James Scott, would recognise his street's character, be pleased by the scale of the new buildings, and bemused by motor cars.

See also: *Bothwell Street* from page 130.

Bothwell Street east from no.95, corner of Blythswood Street.

Lobby in 95 Bothwell Street.

Three buses will come at the one time!

Above: Bothwell Chambers terrace of offices and showrooms, the street's first buildings, started from Hope Street. Its western end was built upon by the bank in the 1930s.

Left: Bothwell Street and corner with Wellington Street.

Below left and right: Bothwell Street connected the city centre and the west-end.

Above: The Central Agency building of J & P Coats Ltd, controlling the world-wide sales of thread.

Right: View over Bothwell Street, up to and beyond St Vincent Street buildings.

Left: Allan House on left. The white sandstone building on the corner of Wellington Street replaced the Glasgow Conservative Club.

The red-sandstoned Mercantile Chambers and adjacent City Line offices are followed by no. 95, Scottish Legal Life Assurance, centre. Mercantile Chambers' archways at street level were intended for an arcade.

SHIPPING WORLD

Of over 70 shipping companies in the city some major ones moved their headquarters to Bothwell Street including the Donaldson Line, State Line, Allan Line (after whom Allan House is named) and the City Line. The mighty Allan Line had so many passenger liners sailing the Atlantic Ocean to Canada and South America that the French government asked them to fly their red, white and blue tricolour ensign a different way – French ships were being confused!

The City Line focussed their passenger cargo liners on the Near East with routes across the Mediterranean and the Indian Ocean.

Above right: City Line's *SS City of York*.
Right: Allan Line's *RMS Alsatian*, to later change its colours and name to *Empress of France* after the merger with Canadian Pacific.

Above: Panorama of Bothwell Street, with Blythswood Street descending.

Right: 95 Bothwell Street – Scottish Legal Life Assurance building – gloriously illuminated.

THE ALBANY HOTEL

In 1973 the exquisite Albany Hotel opened and stole the crown off the Central Hotel. Built by Strand Hotels, part of the food empire of J. Lyons & Co, Trust House Forte took over and maintained the highest of standards.

Part of the Albany Hotel front lobby.

The ballroom and function suites also had a grand entrance from Douglas Street.

It also hosted the St Andrew's Sporting Club whose regular boxing – and championship nights – were often televised. Club nights were all black-tie occasions and after dinner, at tables around the ballroom, coffee was served while boxing got underway.

In the late 1990s a speculative company took over and downgraded it. The function trade moved elsewhere. Its vast site today is occupied by two office blocks, one fronting Waterloo Street and the other fronting Bothwell Street.

A corner of the Four Seasons restaurant.

Above: View from Douglas Street showing 177 Bothwell Street – the latest new office building to open.

Left: Impression of no. 177's roof terrace and running track, with views for those resting.

DOUGLAS STREET

Douglas Street carries the name of the Douglas family, interlinked with the Campbell family. Robert Douglas had married Isabel Elphinstone, the inheritor of the Lands of Blythswood. In essence the (later) Campbells of Blythswood were Douglases, bearing the Douglas crest, right.

Very pleasantly it ambles through Blythswood Square. Douglas Street's own southern flank is surrounded today by glass-fronted office blocks.

A connecting street north/south, Douglas Street has the distinction of having the steepest incline on Blythswood Hill, north of Bothwell Street. Handrails were added, and continue, to help pedestrians up and down it. Horses avoided it.

Above: Douglas Street houses stepping down to St Vincent Street.

Left: Stylish Douglas Street corner with Blythswood Square, but its past owners declining stone-cleaning.

Above: View from Garnethill of Douglas Street beyond Sauchiehall Street, its copper dome, and passing through Blythswood Square.

Below: The copper-domed extension to Bath Street is part of the City of Glasgow Friendly Society founded by John Stewart, celebrated in sculpture. The society continues as Scottish Friendly, based in Blythswood Square.

ELMBANK STREET

Elmbank Street, connecting Sauchiehall Street and St Vincent Street, takes its name from the Elm Bank Place development of the 1830s from St Vincent Street.

A short street, full of purpose. The strong winds off the Clyde make it healthy, but can be stormy when you turn a corner. Patiently on their pedestals of the former high school, Cicero, Homer, Galileo and Watt look forward to the wise redevelopment of their 180 year old academic site.

Elmbank Gardens play host to Charing Cross Station with its trains to and from the Wild West, such as Partick and Helensburgh.

See also: *Bothwell Street* from page 130 and *Elmbank Crescent and its cousins* from page 152.

Above: Elmbank Street looking north to Bath Street and then to Sauchiehall Street.

Right: The west side of Elmbank Street, with Elmbank Crescent joining at Scottish Opera's building.

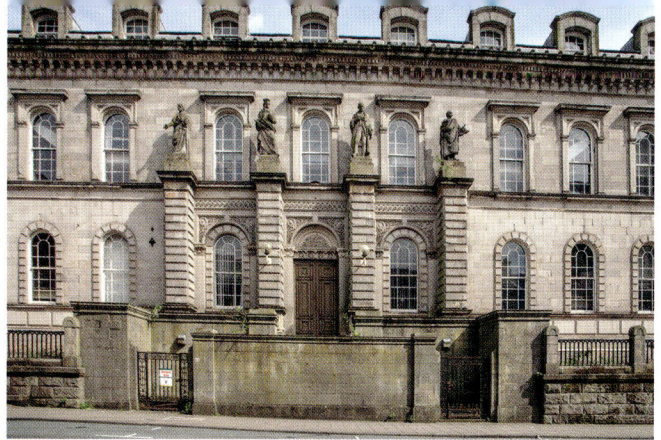

South to St Vincent Street and its futuristic towers, with Cicero, Homer, Galileo and Watt looking on from the school thanks to sculptor John Mossman.

Below: From above Elmbank Gardens, Charing Cross Station shines below and the Mitchell Library beckons beyond.

GORDON STREET

Gordon Street recalls the Gordon family whose mansion house in Buchanan Street viewed west along the future street. Their country pile, Aitkenhead House, continues in King's Park.

The north side of Gordon Street is in Blythswood estates. On the south side, Central Station stands on land owned by the Alston family (related by marriage to the Gordons) direct descendants of John Miller, after whom Miller Street is named. He had developed the district of Grahamston now cleared away by the Central.

Gordon Street's mercantile buildings were joined by fine tea-rooms and function rooms including the Grosvenor on its north side opposite Central Station, and the Ca'Doro on its south at the corner of Union Street.

Glasgow's principal city-centre streets with palaces of commerce and elegant architecture are akin to Venice, especially on a rainy day!

See also: *Bothwell Street* from page 130.

CALEDONIAN RAILWAY COMPANY'S CENTRAL STATION HOTEL, GLASGOW.
Illustrated Souvenir, with Tariff, sent upon application to S. H. Qoser, Hotel Manager.

Above: Caledonian Railway postcard style for use of hotel guests. *Below*: Gordon Street in splendour, from Hope Street.

Left: Looking over Central Station concourse, 1930s.

Below: Viewing along Gordon Street from Hope Street around 1914.

Right: The Grosvenor's main function room and ballroom, Gordon Street.

Below: Gordon Street west to Hope Street and its Central Chambers.

MARBLE STAIRCASE. "THE GROSVENOR". GLASGOW.

Left: Marble staircase of the Grosvenor, Gordon Street.

Below: More sunshine and architectural pleasure.

HILL STREET

Hill Street is like a different world, a geography lesson through time.

David Smith's map of 1828 on page 213 shows Garnet Hill, partly laid out by William Harley. Its first main streets are **Renfrew Street** and, above that, **Hill Street**. This runs along the top of the long hill and looks south and north at the same time.

Its garden villas were joined in the 1850s by very grand tenements. Buccleuch Street and West Graham Street, originally named Graeme Street, were added on the north-facing slopes beyond Hill Street. Families prospering in Cowcaddens moved up hill and up-market to Garnethill.

At the western end is the fine Garnethill Synagogue, the first purpose-built synagogue in Scotland. On the other side, the pioneering Beatson Cancer Hospital, first in Scotland, has apartments within it following the hospital's move to Great Western Road at Gartnavel.

See also: *Promoting the Observatory* from page 48.

Above: One of many villas built on Garnet Hill.

Below: Peel Terrace and other tenements on Hill Street viewing east.

Top left: At the west end of Hill Street, looking towards Woodlands Hill across St George's Road.

Top right: Glasgow Collegiate School, built in 1840.

Above: Hill Street at the junction of Garnethill Street, with the Campsies in the distance.

Right: Formal entrance to St Aloysius College school, built about 1883.

Far right: Good soil, sunshine and a tenement.

HOLLAND STREET

Holland Street is a connection from Sauchiehall Street to St Vincent Street linking with the original small Holland Place development from St Vincent Street of the 1830s. It is not known why the Anderston developers chose the name, perhaps after the prominent politician Lord Holland.

Grown from the ravine west of Blythswood Square, it is settled towards Sauchiehall Street and awaits its new southern half.

Left: Holland Street viewing north to Bath Street and Sauchiehall Street. The high school buildings through to Elmbank Street look forward to their conservation and new uses.

Below: Main gates of high school.

Left: Beyond St Jude's Church built in Jane Street (West George Street, Blythswood Square) stood villas and tenements of Holland Street, past vacant ground in Pitt Street. Etching by Alexander P. Thomson in the 1910s.

Left and below: Spanning Holland Street and Pitt Street, the former Strathclyde Police Headquarters have been razed recently for housing. (West Regent Street hotels are reflected in the glass.) The new housing in progress includes rooftop and courtyard gardens as a respectful nod to William Harley.

HOPE STREET

Hope Street name is in honour of Admiral Sir George Johnston Hope, who served with distinction, alongside Admiral Nelson, throughout the French Revolutionary and Napoleonic Wars. He became captain of the Royal Navy's Baltic Fleet, ensuring the Baltic Sea would finally reopen to British trade. It was first known as Copenhagen Street after earlier successes in forestalling the Danish navy from coming under Napoleon's control.

A street of commerce and supply. In spite of its canyons of fine Victorian architecture rising northwards to West George Street, Hope Street did not attract the postcard photographers who followed the crowds in Sauchiehall Street and Renfield Street.

Above: Central Chambers, Hope Street at Bothwell Street.

Below: Hope Street looking north from Waterloo Street.

Left: S.S. Clan Robertson.

CLAN LINE and OCEAN LIFE

Financed by Glasgow businessmen and shipbuilder Alexander Stephen, the Clan Line was well underway by the 1880s, managed by Charles Cayzer and his sons. The Clan Line soon expanded across every ocean, directed from its headquarters in Central Chambers, 109 Hope Street. In 1918 it bought the Scottish Shire Line, engaged in the refrigerated meat trade with New Zealand and Australia, from Sir James Caird of Glasgow. With the proceeds, Caird became the founder and funder of the National Maritime Museum in Greenwich. By 1938 the Clan Line was the largest cargo-carrying shipping line in the world.

Although Britain's ship-owning companies have given way to global ownerships, the importance of ship-management companies has grown. British and international ship-management companies in Glasgow have significant reach on behalf of global client companies and their maritime trading.

They employ some 200,000 officers, crew and specialists in the technical management, navigation and services for fleets worldwide involved in shipping, offshore and defence industries.

Glasgow continues its long tradition in educating and training more nautical students than any other city in the United Kingdom. From its advanced Riverside Campus, the City of Glasgow College each year produces over one third of all graduate deck officers and marine engineers in Britain, many coming from overseas countries.

Far left: New offices in 1896 with townhouse on the right in St Vincent Street, and on the left the side of Bothwell Chambers of Bothwell Street.

Left: Hope Sreet from Bath Street to Cowcaddens, with the Theatre Royal's tower ahead.

Right: East side of
Hope Street from West
George Street.

Below: West side of
Hope Street from West
George Street.

Left: Top of Hope Street at Cowcaddens, on left is the Theatre Royal which opened in 1867.

Below: Hope Street at night, with St Vincent Street.

PITT STREET

William Pitt

Pitt Street is named after the progressive Prime Minister William Pitt, the Younger.

It started northward from Argyle Street as part of a planned expansion of Blythswood New Town, closer to Anderston. For years the top end next to Sauchiehall Street was equally known as Elgin Place.

Above right: Corner of Bath Street and Pitt Street in different architectural styles.

Below: From Sauchiehall Street, Pitt Street was originally Elgin Place.

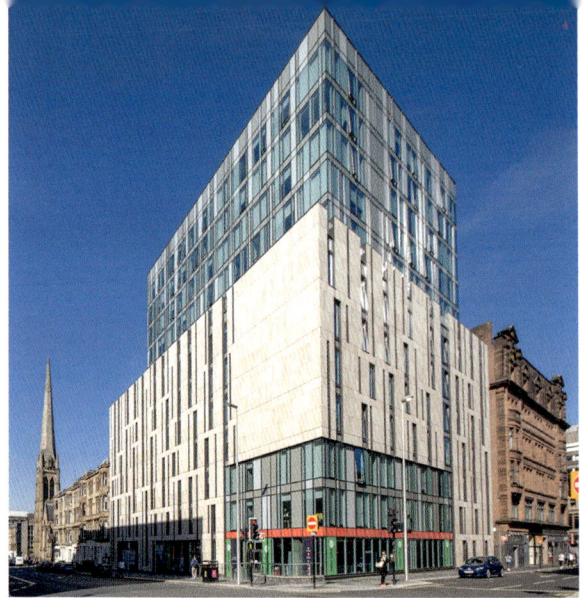

Above: Pitt Street climbing up at Bothwell Street past the quality offices on the left and St Vincent Street Church on the right.

Left: Pitt Street first started from Argyle Street. It was truncated in the early 1970s by the new brutalist Anderston Centre, which today is much reduced.

RENFIELD STREET

Connecting Sauchiehall Street with Argyle Street, through Union Street, and Jamaica Bridge over the Clyde to the southside, the street soon blossomed with shops and offices.

Renfield Street is the main north/south route of Blythswood New Town. It is named after the Campbells' former mansion house of Renfield, down the Clyde at Renfrew, which was cleared to make way for Blythswood House.

Renfield Street and Gordon Street set standards. Up-market stores and tailoring establishments such as RW Forsyth, Carswell and Kirsop were joined by venues offering tea, films and variety. Today it is an artery beloved by buses.

Left: Renfield Street at Gordon Street. Centre left, next to Forsyth's, the white building is the successor to Cranston's De Luxe picture house.

Above: Rising toward West Regent Street with Castle Chambers centre.

Left: Viewing down to St Vincent Street from West George Street.

Renfield Street in the 1900s, approaching St Vincent Street.

TEA and TALKIES

Glasgow created tearooms. Ranges of meals were served throughout the day. One of the pioneers, tea merchant Stuart Cranston, added 13 Renfield Street to his venues. Soon he had the building remodelled to include the Cranston de Luxe picture house, complete with orchestra to accompany the silent films. His younger sister Kate Cranston opened her own artistic tearooms. Talkies started in the late 1920s, Renfield Street having four major cinemas, the fourth being the Regent.

The Paramount, later named Odeon, arrived in Art Deco style, with tearooms throughout. It also had complete theatre stage facilities with frequent concerts by visiting bands and singers from Britain and America. Major new films were exhibited in full in trade shows open to guests after 10.30pm, and often glittering occasions, before national circulation started.

At the top of Renfield Street, Green's Playhouse picture house opened, luxuriously seating over 4,000 patrons – the largest cinema in Europe. Above the picture house was Green's Playhouse ballroom, the largest dance floor in Scotland. It was open six days a week with dancing each afternoon and evening. The ballroom held 1,500 dancers, and 500 spectators in the balconies around it. Green's abounded with tearooms and function rooms. Its site today is the Cineworld tower of screens.

One of three tearooms in the Paramount Odeon picture house.

Above: Renfield Street from the Art Deco frontage of the former Paramount Odeon picture house.

Left: The top of Renfield Street at Renfrew Street in the 1900s, with the newly opened Pavilion Theatre on the right.

RENFIELD STREET, FROM PAVILION, GLASGOW.

RENFREW STREET

Renfrew Street reflects the royal burgh of Renfrew where the Campbells of Blythswood had extensive land.

It is the better known of the two main streets on Garnet Hill, so named by William Harley. The other is **Hill Street**, once complete with Observatory.

To its early garden villas and terraces, Renfrew Street attracted commercial buildings and colleges. These include the Glasgow Dental Hospital and School in the 1930s, morphing to a modern tower block on Sauchiehall Street; Glasgow School of Art; and the Royal Scottish Academy of Music and Drama, moving up from Buchanan Street in the 1980s, and now named the Royal Conservatoire of Scotland.

In the 1900s the School of Art climbed uphill from its nearby home in the McLellan Galleries, Sauchiehall Street. Its exquisite Art Nouveau building designed by architect Charles Rennie Mackintosh, and unique in the world, epitomised design and art in the industries and culture of Glasgow. The institution added more buildings to its stock. In the 21st century two successive fires hollowed the masterpiece Glasgow School of Art building under the watch of the institution. Its governors have stated that the building will be rebuilt to Mackintosh's design and standards.

Above: Glasgow School of Art, designed by Charles Rennie Mackintosh.

Far left: Art School student fashion design on display in Scott Street, looking down to Sauchiehall Street, 1953.

Left: Glasgow School of Art, west gable.

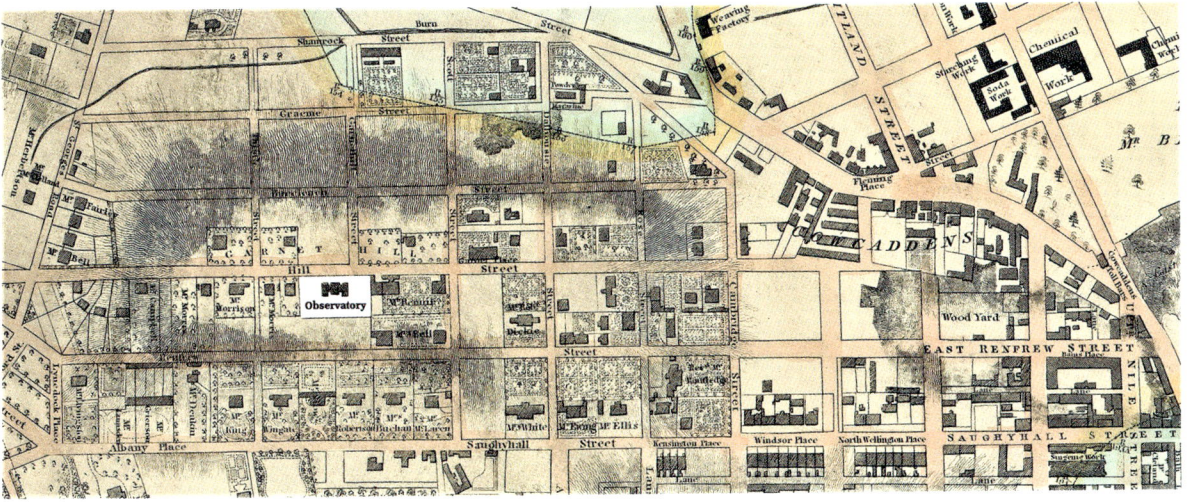

Top: Garnet Hill mapped by David Smith, 1828.

Above: Royal Conservatoire of Scotland, entered from Renfrew Street at the corner of Hope Street.

Left: Housing in Renfrew Street, viewing west.

ST. VINCENT STREET

St Vincent Street celebrates the naval victory in 1797 in the Atlantic Ocean off Cape St. Vincent, Portugal, during the French Revolutionary Wars. Led by Admiral Jervis (later Earl St Vincent), the Royal Navy defeated the larger Spanish fleet which was on its way to combine with the French fleet.

St Vincent Place, just east of Buchanan Street, is the main link from George Square New Town to Blythswood New Town west of Buchanan Street.

Like West George Street above it and Gordon Street and Bothwell Street below it, St Vincent Street has a brilliance of architecture, but on a monumental scale, which speaks of the wealth of Glasgow and the reach of its commerce and banking. Classical and modern reflect its confidence.

See also: *First New Houses* from page 86 and *The Blair Family and 242 St Vincent Street* from page 94.

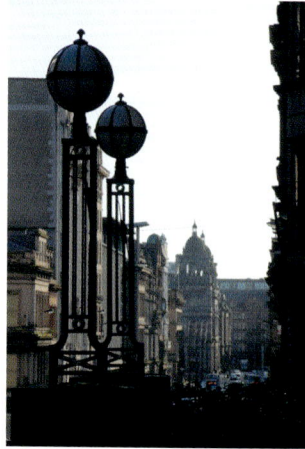

Left: Dawn from 145 St Vincent Street.

Below: St Vincent Street's headquarter buildings include no. 151's glass cascades, reflecting compatriots across the road.

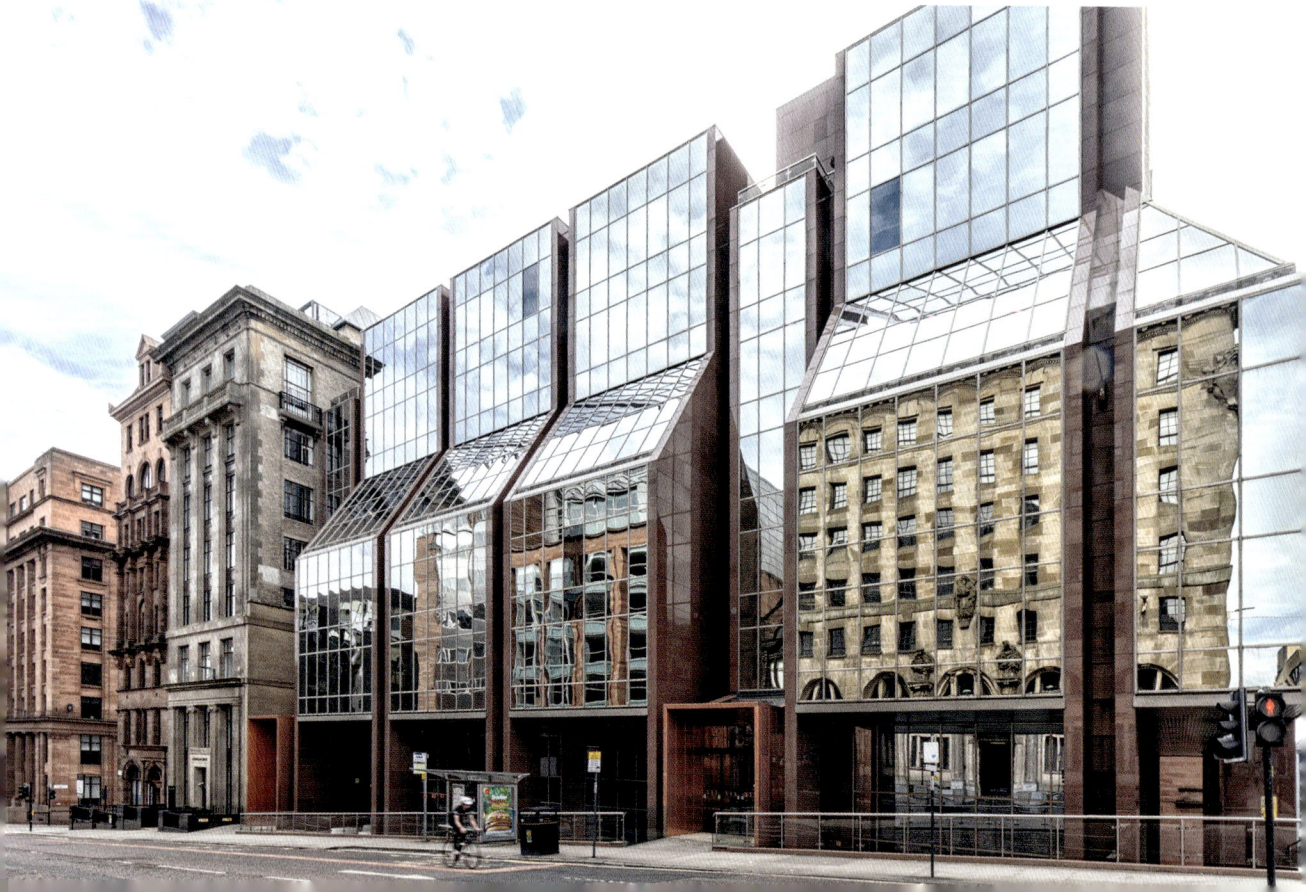

Below: St Vincent Place, photographed in the 1890s, connects George Square and St Vincent Street on its journey westward.

Bottom: St Vincent Street rises to Blythswood Hill and, right, West Nile Street climbing to the site of William Harley's baths and pioneering dairy.

Looking back along St Vincent Street from Elmbank Street.

ARCHITECTS

Early architects of the first order in Glasgow and across the country, such as David Hamilton – from the 1790s onwards – William Stark and John Baird were soon joined by John Burnet, snr, Charles Wilson, Hugh Barclay, John Honeyman, John Thomas Rochhead, Charles Wilson, Alexander Kirkland, William Leiper, Thomas Lennox Watson, and by Alexander 'Greek' Thomson, prolific and prominent in buildings and interior design.

He was surpassed by a younger rival, Sir John James Burnet, nationally the most famous of all in his lifetime. By this time, other major innovation came from James Sellars, John Keppie, James Miller, James Salmon, jnr, and Charles Rennie Mackintosh with his blending of exteriors with all aspects of interior design. Later architects have added their stamp.

In recent decades, new construction is required to be behind existing facades of the Conservation Area or be of a height and finish which respects its neighbours.

Sandstones and finishes in fine array, the Union Bank of Scotland prominent at the corner of Renfield Street.

UNION BANK OF SCOTLAND

From around George Square and Buchanan Street, Glasgow's banking and insurance headquarters developed along St Vincent Street. Life assurance also blossomed. In 1927 the well-established Union Bank of Scotland opened its new headquarters at 110 St Vincent Street. The bank's general manager Norman Hird and architect James Miller had visited Chicago and New York looking at latest developments, particularly the architecture of banks on Wall Street.

The bank's spaciousness and Art Deco styling exuded confidence. It operated in the manner that Glasgow expected. The Union Bank's chairman Sir Steven Bilsland, Norman Hird and convenor Sir Cecil Weir were the driving force behind the successful Empire Exhibition, 1938, in Bellahouston Park attracting 13 million visitors.

In the 1950s the Union Bank and the older Bank of Scotland merged under the chairmanship of Lord Bilsland of the Union Bank. Both firms were about the same size.

Until the collapse of the Bank of Scotland in 2008, the Glasgow Chief Office at 110 St Vincent Street was normally the busiest and most commercially successful of all Bank of Scotland sites in the United Kingdom.

In all cities the digital revolution continues to mean many splendid banking halls and insurance halls now serve hospitality in place of pounds.

Above left: Lobby entrance to the banking hall; counters on the left (out of view).

Above right: Aerial view over the Empire Exhibition, 1938. Mosspark Boulevard in foreground.

Left top: Between Renfield and Hope Street, offices built for life assurance and inurance firms have been remodelled behind their facades. In the centre front basement was the Ivy restaurant.

Below left: Viewing east along St Vincent Street from Hope Street.

Right: 145 St Vincent Street, also known as the Stenhouse building, at Wellington Street; reflections from across the road.

Below: West from Hope Street to Wellington Street, the street here was built in the 1810s as Blythswood Place. See illustration on page 86.

Above: 219-245 St Vincent Street on the south side, opposite the Royal College.

Far left: The Royal College of Physicians and Surgeons of Glasgow.

Left: Hallway of one of the townhouses which comprise the Royal College.

Left: Looking west downhill from the corner of Douglas Street.

Opposite above: 200 St Vincent Street designed by Sir John James Burnet in the 1920s; on the corner with West Campbell Street.

Opposite below: 206-226 St Vincent Street remodelled around 1900 creating the Institute of Chartered Accountants' library and rooms in the centre with its lecture halls on left.

Above: St Vincent Street Church and tenement designed by Alexander Thomson; Unitarian Chapel beyond; and St Columba Church on right.

Left: Alexander 'Greek' Thomson's masterful St Vincent Street Church opened in 1859.

Top: Inside St Vincent Street Church.

Above: Unitarian Church opened in 1855; Bothwell Street behind, Terrace Street to right.

Left: View from Bothwell Street.

Sumptious offices opening in 1986 for the British National Oil Corporation (Britoil); now occupied by a banking corporation.

Right: St Columba Church of Scotland, equally known as the Gaelic Church.

Below: St Vincent Street viewing east from North Street.

SAUCHIEHALL STREET

Sauchiehall Street name echoes the sauch-lined haugh through which ran a country road to Partick.

In its heyday from the 1880s to the 1970s Sauchiehall Street was world famous for its art and galleries, deluxe tearooms, boutiques and the most elegant of stores such as Copland & Lye, Pettigrew & Stephens, Trérons, Daly's, Andrew Muirhead and Alexander Henderson's. It had numerous ballrooms, dance halls and half a dozen cinemas in or just off the street.

At the far western end, beyond Charing Cross, are Kelvingrove Park and the mighty Kelvingrove Art Galleries & Museum.

Despite its decline and the mothballing of the splendid McLellan Galleries the street still has entertainment venues nearby including the King's Theatre (Bath Street), Glasgow Film Theatre (Rose Street), Theatre Royal (Hope Street) and Pavilion Theatre (Renfield Street). Round a corner to Renfrew Street is the premier academy for music, drama and dance – the Royal Conservatoire of Scotland. Its venues and Athenaeum Theatre have public performances throughout the year. At the eastern end of Sauchiehall Street is the Royal Concert Hall, viewing down Buchanan Street.

See also: *First New Houses* from page 86.

Below: Sauchiehall Street westwards from the top of Buchanan Street around 1900, with the Empire Theatre centre left at West Nile Street. St John's Methodist Church is on the right.

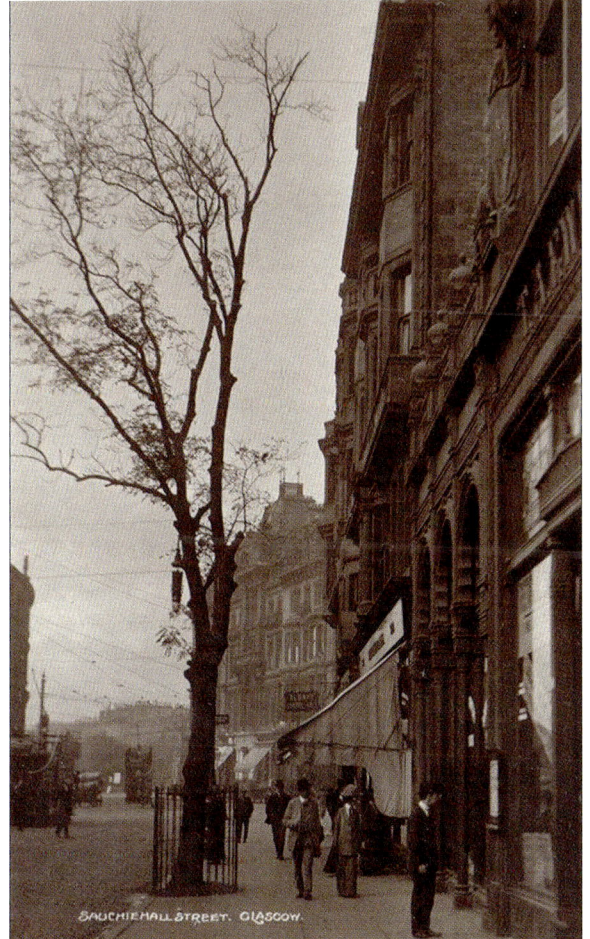

Top: Sauchiehall Street today viewing west from the top of Buchanan Street at the Royal Concert Hall.

Above: Pedestrianisation starts, Sauchiehall Street at Rose Street, 1970s.

Right: Pavement view and willow tree in Sauchiehall Street at Charing Cross, 1900s.

Right: Sauchiehall Street viewing east from Charing Cross, about 1900.

Below: Alexander Thomson's Grecian Chambers was bought with the proceeds of the sale of the Lady Artists' Club, Blythswood Square, and is an art centre; originally the Third Eye Centre and now the Contemporary Centre for Arts.

SAUCHIEHALL STREET, GLASGOW.

Above: A usual busy day in Sauchiehall Street, taken from Hope Street, 1930s. On the left, and westwards, is where William Harley built his first housing for sale on Blythswood, in the 1810s.

Left: The McLellan Galleries building, Sauchiehall Street, viewed from Douglas Street.

Above: The Salon de Luxe in the Willow Tearooms of Kate Cranston, designed by Charles Rennie Macintosh.

Left: Sauchiehall Street Christmas lights in 1962. Just like Argyle Street and George Square, these were in glorious colours, but photographed here in newspaper black and white.

CHARING CROSS, GLASGOW

Civilised transport. Glasgow's tram network, electrified in 1900, became the second largest in Britain, only slightly smaller than London's.

WATERLOO STREET

Waterloo Street, starting from Hope Street, celebrates the military victory at Waterloo in the Low Countries in 1815 when Britain and the allies finally defeated Napoleon Bonaparte, and ended France's empire of Europe.

On the level and active. Central Station is a handy neighbour.

See also: *Bothwell Street* from page 130.

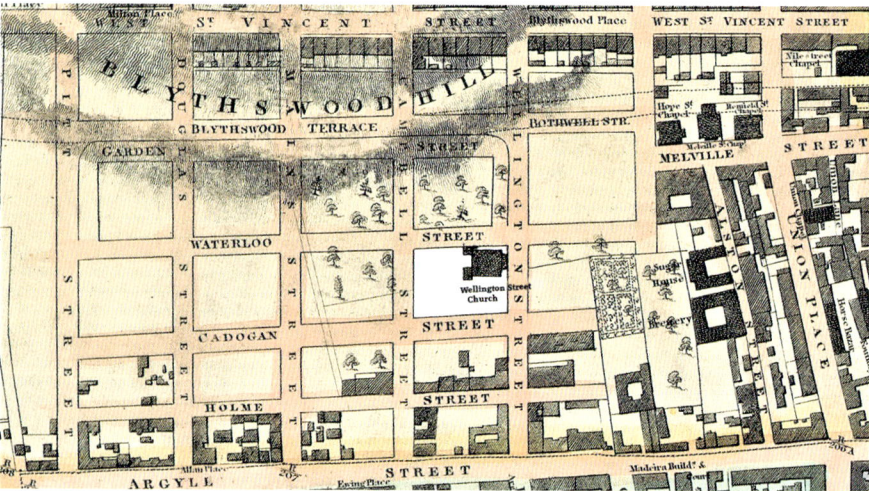

Left: Map of 1828 showing Wellington Street Church at the corner of Waterloo Street, while most streets await development. Melville Street became Gordon Street.

Above: Alhambra House stretching west along Waterloo Street, on left is Wellington Street.

Left: Waterloo Street Parcels sorting office of the GPO has been converted to offices.

Top left: Waterloo Chambers, opened in 1899, continues today. One of many innovative designs by Sir John James Burnet.

Top right: Waterloo Street, and its taxi rank, drawing by Robert Eadie, 1925.

Opposite, clockwise from top right: Alhambra Theatre, painting by Robert Eadie, 1927; Auditorium from the stage; Demolition from the stage; Arriving for a *Five Past Eight* show.

THE ALHAMBRA

The Alhambra Theatre, opening in 1910 at the corner of Wellington Street and Waterloo Street where Wellington Street Church once stood, took the lead in variety with plays, opera and ballet on the bills. It was luxuriously moderne, anticipating Art Deco, and designed by architect Sir John James Burnet.

Under its founder Sir Alfred Butt it added pantomime, long running musicals, seasons of plays, full scale opera and ballet. From the 1950s the famed and fast-moving *Five Past Eight Shows* each summer presented glamour, music, song and comedy with changes of programme each fortnight and then each four weeks for up to six months of the year. The most profitable of theatres.

The latest building on its site, Alhambra House, is finished in style and quality, fitting of the Alhambra.

WELLINGTON STREET

Duke of Wellington.

Wellington Street marks the name of the Duke of Wellington, a son of Dublin, statesman and commander-in-chief of the British Army which brought the long-running Napoleonic Wars to an end. He was a soldiers' soldier and cared greatly for his men. In later years he became Prime Minister.

Wellington and West Campbell Streets are of similar interest and convenience.

Of the many theatres built in Glasgow, over twenty, the most successful, and the best equipped in Britain, was the Alhambra, opening in 1910 in Wellington Street at the corner of Waterloo Street (which see).

Wellington Street cascading south towards Argyle Street.

Left: Wellington meets Waterloo – famous names.

Below: Wellington Street's extensive Baltic Chambers in baltic sunshine.

WEST CAMPBELL STREET

West Campbell Street is named for the Campbells, owners of the Lands of Blythswood from the later 17th century, through political intrigue within the city council. In essence they were Douglases first and foremost.

The continuation of West Campbell Street north of Sauchiehall Street – interrupted now by pedestrianisation – is Cambridge Street, where William Harley and some of his family lived in a villa after moving from Willow Bank.

Of the many connecting streets of Blythswood, from north to south, West Campbell Street, like its neighbour Wellington Street, provides a good walk with quieter traffic. And a visual feast when crossing over all the major streets from east to west on Blythswood Hill. Down hill or up hill. Hostelries at both ends offer rest.

West Campbell Street rising from Waterloo Street.

Above: North from its plateau to Bath Street, and beyond Sauchiehall Street.

Right: South to West George Street, then down towards Argyle Street.

WEST GEORGE STREET

George Street itself descends from High Street and past George Square to Buchanan Street at St George's Church. When St George's opened in 1808 it was 'on the edge of the country'.

West George Street, starting in the 1810s from the new 'Nile Street', extends west from the original George Street named in honour of King George III who reigned for 59 years.

With its distinguished air, West George Street has a fine palette of commercial palazzos and townhouses rising to Blythswood Square.

West George Street glides up Blythswood Hill to Blythswood Square.

Above: Looking to West Nile Street, where the New Town of Blythswood started, and to St George's Tron Church. Centre left is the Venetian building of the Royal Faculty of Procurators of Glasgow.

Left: Pallazos and townhouses in West George Street.

CITY CENTRE CLUBS

In the city centre, by the end of the 19th century, there were now about a dozen clubs of some wealth, with their own premises. Nearly all were for gentlemen sharing interests in business, politics or art – or any combination of them! They followed the lead of the first, the Western Club in 1842, whose building continues at the corner of Buchanan Street and St Vincent Street. The club is now in Royal Exchange Square. The Glasgow Art Club opened up in Bath Street. Glasgow Literary Club, nearby in St Vincent Street, had its counterpoint in the Glasgow Society of Musicians' Club in Berkely Street, adding a Concert Room (now café/restaurant).

West George Street saw the elegant New Club (right), designed by James Sellars, open its doors at numbers 144-146 in 1880. (Wives and sisters were shown around it the day before it opened to members.) Others included the Merchants Club emerging in Royal Exchange Square, the Junior Club in Sauchiehall Street at Charing Cross – including outdoor tennis courts – and the Conservative Club in Bothwell Street. The Liberal Club began in style at the corner of Buchanan Street and St George's Place. Its building remains open today after being adopted by the Scottish Academy of Music & Drama – next door to the continuing Athenaeum which was open to all. Members of the German Club (Deutscher Verein), founded in the 1860s in Sauchiehall Street, were naturalised citizens but, later in Bath Street, closed the club after the sinking of the *Lusitania* in 1915.

Two clubs opened for ladies. The Glasgow Society of Lady Artists in 1882, moving in the 1890s to Blythswood Square as the Lady Artists' Club. The second club for ladies was the Kelvin Club in 1897, soon opening in Buchanan Street, and named after one of its founders, Lady Kelvin.

NEW CLUB GLASGOW.

MESSRS CAMPBELL DOUGLAS AND SELLARS, ARCHITECTS

Top: West George Street with the New Club premises centre left.

CUNARD

Samuel Cunard from Canada was keen to win the first contract for Royal Mail services between Britain and America. He was consulting with Robert Napier of Glasgow. But he had no ships nor funds for the frequency and speed he required. He came to London looking for steamships and funding to find there was little interest there, nor knowledge of the new technologies. He was advised to go to Glasgow.

When he arrived in the city in 1839 he had dinner that evening in the West George Street house of shipowner George Burns. In the morning he had breakfast with marine engineer Robert Napier in his house in Anderston's Bothwell Street. The Cunard Line was born!

The majority of shares were held by Scots, chiefly Burns and his associates. The first secretary was a nephew of Jane Laird, the late Mrs William Harley. In its 160 years based in Britain most of Cunard's chairmen and leading directors were Scots. Most of its ships, including the largest in the world, were built on the Clyde. Today, Cunard is owned by a firm in the USA.

Top: Looking west from Hope Street.

Above: The commanding new offices at 191 West George Street include the townhouse site of no.195 at the corner with Wellington Street.

Left: A classical townhouse at no. 198, built in the 1820s.

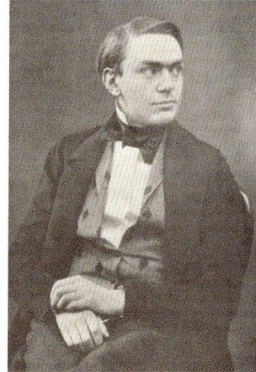

Far left: 195 West George Street, extended as Nobel House around 1900.

Left: Alfred Nobel at the age of thirty, a few years before he co-founded the British Dynamite Company.

CHEMICALS, EXPLOSIVES and STEEL

Charles Tennant, previously a weaver from Glenconner farm in Ayrshire, built his family townhouse at 195 West George Street in 1830. He had become a chemist and jointly with Charles Macintosh patented their invention of bleaching powder and other chemicals which became essential to the textile and metal industries. Moving from Darnley, they created the St Rollox Chemical Works, and built the largest chemical company in the world.

The Tennants were active in public reform and in national politics. Gladstone became a visitor to the house on his campaigns, addressing crowds from the front steps. As a wealthy and artistic family they had a ballroom on the first floor, the front and full breadth of the house. A Tennant daughter became the wife of Prime Minister Asquith.

From 1900 their West George Street townhouse became the new headquarters of Nobel Explosives Ltd, formed in Glasgow in the 1870s as the British Dynamite Company. At its creation, Alfred Nobel was joint equal owner with a group of Glasgow industrialists. With its main explosives works on the Ayrshire coast at Ardeer, selected by Nobel himself, the Glasgow company was the largest of the Nobel companies throughout the world.

Sir Charles Tennant, a grandson of the founder, continued to develop St Rollox chemical works and its many products sold worldwide. He became president of Nobel Explosives and of the United Alkali chemical combine in the UK, becoming cornerstones of the new Imperial Chemical Industries group initiated in 1926 and led by Sir Harry McGowan of Pollokshields.

The Tennants were also international metal traders, bankers, owners of gold mines in India, copper mines in Spain and owners of islands in the Caribbean (one fascinating the future Princess Margaret.)

From 1921 the extended house was the headquarters of the Colvilles steel group and its associates for some 50 years before moving to new premises at 120 Bothwell Street.

Left: West George Street met by Wellington Street. John McLeod, architect of the centre classical building, designed similar stylish warehouses for Simons, Jacob & Co., fruit brokers, and Garnethill Synagogue where the Simons were leading members.

Below: West George Street terraces of townhouses on the hill have changed little from the 1820s.

Right: Beyond the square, West George Street started as Jane Street, named after the daughter of developer H.W.Garden.

Below: Much of the sandstone used in building Blythswood came from the Eastwood Quarries, which extended to Giffnock. The quarries were owned by Robert McHaffie who had a townhouse in Blythswood Square.

Bottom right: St Jude's Church, built in 1839, is now the entrance and central part of a hotel.

WEST NILE STREET

West Nile Street (originally named Nile Street) marks the victory of the Royal Navy in 1798 in the Mediterranean during the French Republican Wars. In secret, Napoleon Bonaparte attempted to land his armies in Egypt and from there strike out against British India. Under Admiral Nelson, the navy surprised and routed the French navy at Aboukir Bay.

It is a comfortable backwater, sandwiched between Buchanan Street and Renfield Street and its slope is kinder than its westerly neighbours.

Buchanan Street railway station and its mineral sidings, operated by the Caledonian Railway company, opened in 1849 at the top of West Nile Street – where Glasgow Caledonian University now stands. To help carters with heavy loads get up the hill, trace horses from John Wordie & Company's haulage stables nearby were always stationed at the foot of West Nile Street. Attended by the trace boys, the Clydesdales would be added, making a double harness. Many legs make light work!

See also: *Harley's Baths in Bath Street* from page 58.

Left: West Nile Street and sociable venues.

Below: West Nile Street viewing north from Gordon Street. The Lands of Blythswood started from here, with the Enoch Burn flowing down to the Clyde.

Left: Trace horses at the foot of West Nile Street, painting by Robert Eadie, 1930s.

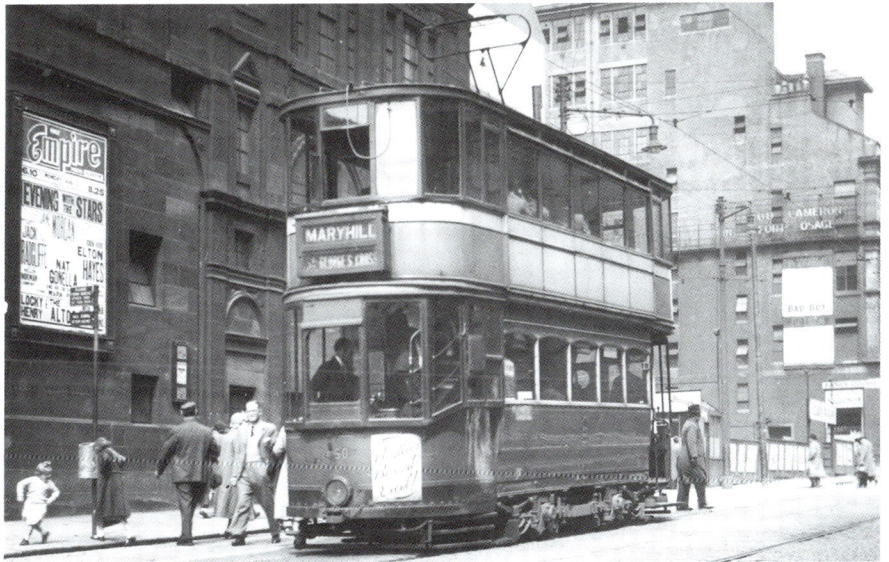

Right: Tram stop, alight here at the West Nile Street stagedoor of the Empire Theatre, Sauchiehall Street.

Left: Trolley buses took over some of the city's tram routes, increasingly in the 1950s.

Right: North from West George Street.

Below: West Nile Street from left to right at West George Street, showing architecture across 200 years.

Above: West Nile Street crossing over Bath Street, where William Harley started new ventures in providing water, baths, hygienic milk and baking. The rows of shops await development.

Right: Looking south from the top of West Nile Street.

WEST REGENT STREET

West Regent Street or Regent Street as it was first known, takes its title from the Prince Regent – George, Prince of Wales – who, in 1811, took up the regency of his elderly father, King George III.

It is a quieter street than its siblings, mainly content with itself. Possibly this is because it never broke into Buchanan Street. Underneath the full length of West Regent Street runs the busy tunnel of railway lines carrying all the services from Queen Street Low Level station.

At the western end of the street, beyond Blythswood Square, is now a host of hotels and student accommodation. The eastern end,

meeting West Nile Street, has very new tall offices which step down in height to Renfield Street and the Conservation area.

Below: West Regent Street from its start at West Nile Street, with Blythswood Square in the distance.

Top: The Victoria Buildings opened in West Regent Street in 1860, taking up the full block to West Nile Street. Its promoter and owner – John Orr Ewing – the Turkey-red textile magnate, whose headquarters occupied part of the building, was also the founder chairman of Young's Paraffin Oil Company, forerunner of BP.

Above: The Victoria Buildings photographed in the 1860s.

Top: West Regent Street east towards West Nile Street.

Above: Corner of Hope Street and West Regent Street, right, highlights a Queen Anne adaptation in 1905 by James Salmon, with its art nouveau beaten-copper panels and motifs; two of them shown left.

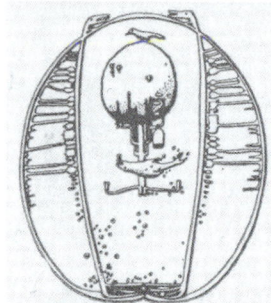

Above: A terrace in its sunny aspect since arrival in the 1830s. William Harley laid out his streets well.

Left: Entrance to Sovereign House.

Top: Now offices, the red sandstoned buildings in West Regent Street at the corner of West Campbell Street, opened as Sovereign House, being The Institute for the Adult Deaf and Dumb; next to which came the John Ross Memorial Church for the Deaf.

Above right: Stop! West Nile Street looking down to Mitchell Street.

Below right: Cross now! West Nile Street at Gordon Street.

Jean (Darroch) & Graeme Smith arrive in the Grosvenor, Gordon Street, for the Glasgow CA Students' Society Annual Ball, 1965.

Acknowledgements

The first thank you is to William Harley (1767-1830). He always had a plan, maybe too many, and he made improvements. We can drink a healthy (Harley) glass of milk to that. He also wrote a book to encourage others to improve.

Special thanks to Mike McCreery of Queens Park Camera Club for new photography and picture-editing. We traipsed up and down the streets and slopes of Blythswood and Garnethill in all seasons while looking up at buildings and across vistas. Jay-walking is in Glasgow veins and we avoided being knocked down by traffic. However, scaffolding and perpetual road-digging bring different challenges! New photography also came from Raymond Forbes, Douglas Lindsay, Damian Russell, Bill Mackintosh, Ian Johnston, Hamish Stevenson, Robert Poole, Gordon Haws, Alan Murray-Rust, Ewan McAndrew, Mark Osborne, Anna Wilson, HFD Group, Radisson Hotel Group, Three Sixty Architecture, Glasgow City Free Church, Scottish Friendly Assurance, Blythswood Square Hotel, and The Willow Tearooms Trust and their photographers Rachel Keenan and Phil Wilkinson.

Organisations and individuals who generously responded to requests for information and assistance include the Mitchell Library, Glasgow City Archives, Glasgow Museums, University of Glasgow Library (especially about historic maps and views), National Records of Scotland, Historic Environment Scotland, Royal College of Physicians and Surgeons of Glasgow, Glasgow Chamber of Commerce, Glasgow Art Club, Royal Scottish Automobile Club, National Trust for Scotland, Watt Institution Greenock, the late Professor Michael Moss, Professor John R. Hume, John Moore, Dr Glenda White, Dr Nick Kuenssberg, Professor Bruce Peter, Priscilla Barlow, Inchinnan Historical Group and the Friends of St Conan's Kirk.

Editing has been enabled by the late Dr Peter V. Davies of Glasgow University, a French linguist, native of Wales and adopted Glaswegian. The book's design is thanks to the artistic smeddum of Shirley Lochhead. Bell & Bain, the book's printers, continue to demonstrate their high standards from 1831 onwards.

Selected reading

Glasgow Past & Present, by Sencx, published in three volumes in 1856. Available online.

An illustrated Guide to Glasgow 1837, by Maurice Lindsay, published in 1989. Written as if you were a visitor in the year 1837.

William Harley, a Citizen of Glasgow, by John Galloway, published in 1901. John Galloway was a colleague of the Harley family. He became head of the shipping line Patrick Henderson & Company and President of Glasgow Chamber of Commerce.

The Harleian Dairy System, by William Harley, published in 1829. Available online.

Men of Iron, The Story of Cammell Laird Shipbuilders 1828-1991, by David Hollett, published in 1992.

The Second City: Glasgow, by Charles Oakley, published 1975 and frequently since.

Glasgow's Gain: The Anderston Story, by Derek Dow and Michael Moss, published in 1986.

Glasgow, by Irene Maver, published in 2000.

Treasures of the College. Celebrating 300 Years of the Library of the Royal College of Physicians and Surgeons of Glasgow, editors James J. Beaton, Roy Miller and Iain T. Boyle, published in 1998.

The Architecture of Glasgow, by Andor H. Gomme and David Walker, published in 1968 and again in 1987.

Mackintosh's Masterwork: The Glasgow School of Art, editor William Buchanan, published in 1989.

Charles Rennie Mackintosh: Architect-Artist-Icon, by John McKean and Colin Baxter, published in 2000.

The Glasgow Boys, by Roger Bilcliffe, latest edition published in 2008.

Glasgow Girls: Women in Art and Design 1880-1920, editor Jude Burkhauser, published in 1990 and since.

Tea and Taste: The Glasgow Tea Rooms 1875-1975, by Perilla Kinchin, published in 1991 and since.

Glasgow's Blythswood Graeme Smith
All rights reserved 2021
Designed and typeset by Shirley Lochhead
Printed in Glasgow by Bell & Bain Ltd.

Blythswood Square gardens, devised by William Harley.